"Larry Crabb is equal parts Bible scholar and professional counselor, which makes him the ideal person to address this topic. And in an era of global terrorism, nuclear fears, political divisions, and devastating natural disasters, we need a trustworthy guide to explore God's ways."

Philip Yancey, bestselling author of *Disappointment with God* and *Where Is God When It Hurts?*

"No matter who you are, at some point you'll encounter a situation where God's plan just doesn't seem to add up. Those are difficult times, and they can truly test your faith. What matters is how you respond. Larry Crabb understands, and he provides practical insights to help us identify and choose the way forward."

Jim Daly, president of Focus on the Family

"From a renowned Christian mentor who has been living in the shadows of his own mortality; he writes biographically and deeply compassionately on behalf of many troubled souls. A wonderful and passionate book!"

James M. Houston, Board of Governors' Professor of Spiritual Theology, Regent College, Vancouver, BC

"I love it when Larry Crabb comes out with a new book. I know I'll be reading something that will profoundly touch my life. *When God's Ways Make No Sense* is that on steroids. Frankly, I don't understand God, His ways, or why He's doing what He's doing in my life and that of those I love. 'Trust and tremble' isn't my normal response to God's ways. Sometimes it's more 'cuss and spit.' This book is profound, fresh, practical, and life-altering. I'm going to be different and better because of it, and you will too!"

Steve Brown, author, broadcaster, and seminary professor

"I have always admired Larry Crabb for his authentic honesty about the challenges of life balanced with an unwavering trust in God's character. Once again, he walks this tightrope well in *When God's Ways Make No Sense*."

Mark McMinn, author of *The Science of Virtue: Why Positive Psychology Matters to the Church*

"Dr. Larry Crabb's latest book will be an encouragement to those Christians who are perplexed over the way God allows things that don't make sense, especially when He is so loving and also all-powerful. Dr. Crabb shows that God's ways are higher than our ways, and His thoughts are higher than ours. The prophet Habakkuk had the same perplexities—and complained to God about them! You will see that you are not the first to not understand God's ways. Habakkuk came through and so will you—especially after you read this book."

R. T. Kendall, pastor, author, and international speaker

"Dr. Crabb has written a must-read guide for every follower of Jesus struggling to understand during difficult and confusing times when God's ways often seem to make no sense."

Dr. Jamie Swalm, cofounder of LargerStory.com

"There are some things we don't talk about. And we need to. Because what we conclude deeply affects the way we relate to God and to one another. I'm talking about unanswered prayer. Pain, Larry Crabb writes, escorts us to a crossroads. Will we choose to trust God's goodness or resist and run? Confronted by tragedy, will we choose to trust God's goodness or reject God's plan for one more to our liking? Dr. Crabb challenges us to explore what it might look like to rest in mystery, to embrace God's grace-filled invitation to trust and persevere, even—and especially—when God's ways make no sense, and to live in certainty that God is writing a beautiful story with our lives. This book is honest, it is important, it is for such a time as this. I urge you, take and read."

Dr. Miriam (Mimi) Dixon, senior pastor of First Presbyterian Church of Golden, Colorado

"Wise guides recognize that living in the status quo rarely leads to change. These guides have a unique capacity to foster growth in others by helping them to feel discomfort. Dr. Crabb's growing wisdom has benefitted many of us. He willingly enters into territory that many of us attempt to avoid. He ventures deep into the obscure darkness and tells us what he sees, both those things that make him tremble in the night and those things that reflect the beauty and goodness of God. He brings us to the edge of discomfort, and sometimes past it, so we might better know the realities of a spiritually forming life."

Jason Kanz, PhD, pastor, board certified clinical neuropsychologist, and author of *Soil of the Divine*

"There may be no more difficult hurdle in the Christian experience than when life and God make no sense. Any honest pilgrim comes face-to-face with this reality. Now what? There are other initially more appealing options, as Dr. Crabb identifies, but only one resonates with our heart of hearts. Once again, Larry invites us to think hard about the unfamiliar and less-traveled road. It may at first appear we've taken a wrong turn, only to discover further down the road that perhaps an obscure prophet's way is life-giving."

Dr. Kent Denlinger, pastor of Valley Springs Fellowship, Warsaw, IN

"Honest Christians will come face-to-face with the reality that God's ways often make no sense. Whether through his books or during a shared cup of coffee, Larry Crabb has been a consistent voice urging me to wrestle with the mystery of living the Christian life. This book is a must-read for any who struggle with God and yet long to trust Him more than understand Him. Larry is a friend, a mentor, and a fellow struggler on the journey."

Jim Kallam, Church at Charlotte, author of *Risking Church*

"Dr. Crabb has captured the essence of God's love that runs so much deeper than our understanding. Throughout the book, Larry is a voice of truth that inspires yet challenges. While reading we contemplated hard questions that we were either unaware we had or unwilling to ask out loud. A must-read if you desire to live anchored in the goodness of God's heart."

Arlita and Butch Ibach, owners of The Red Dot Coffee Company

WHEN GOD'S WAYS MAKE NO SENSE

DR. LARRY CRABB

BakerBooks

a division of Baker Publishing Group
Grand Rapids, Michigan

Published by Baker Books
a division of Baker Publishing Group
PO Box 6287, Grand Rapids, MI 49516-6287
www.bakerbooks.com

Printed in the United States of America

Library of Congress Cataloging-in-Publication Data

Names: Crabb, Larry, 1944– author.
Title: When God's ways make no sense / Dr. Larry Crabb.
Description: Grand Rapids : Baker Publishing Group, 2018. | Includes bibliographical
   references.
Identifiers: LCCN 2017053750 | ISBN 9780801015328 (cloth)
Subjects: LCSH: Trust in God—Christianity. | Suffering—Religious aspects—Christianity.
Classification: LCC BV4637 .C725 2018 | DDC 248.8/6—dc23
LC record available at https://lccn.loc.gov/2017053750

18   19   20   21   22   23   24   7   6   5   4   3   2   1

As we grow older together,
I even more deeply value the love of my wife.
She pays a higher price than anyone
for me to do what I do.
I therefore dedicate this latest effort
to Rachael, my wife of more than fifty years.

What Jonah heard from God made no sense to him.
So Jonah resisted and ran.

What Saul heard from God (before he became Paul) made no
sense to him.
So Saul distorted and denied.

What Habakkuk heard from God made no sense to him.
But Habakkuk trembled and trusted.

Contents

Contents

Acknowledgments

No book is the effort of only its author.

The team at Baker Books provided great help in making this book as good as it could be. Special thanks to my go-to guy, Chad Allen.

Tom and Jenny and Bob and Claudia gave rich and encouraging feedback as they read the manuscript. Now that Rachael and I have left Denver for Charlotte, we miss each of you a lot!

Trip Moore, Jim Kallam, Steve Shores: three friends among others who make me think till confusion gives way to enough clarity to keep pressing on.

Our church family at Golden Presbyterian Church for a decade of love, support, and encouragement; and to Mimi Dixon, pastor, sister, and friend. I miss our breakfasts.

My "little team" of Andi and Kep, who stay close with support, practical help, and meaningful encouragement. My gratitude runs deep.

And Rachael, the real center of our "little team" at New Way Ministries: she is with me as no one else.

Foreword

I first met Larry Crabb in the spring of 2003. His groundbreaking book, *Inside Out*, had made a huge impact on me when I was in seminary in the late 1980s. I couldn't wait to meet this man whose writings had helped me get through some difficult times over the years. One of his sons was attending the church I pastored at that time, and had arranged for us to play a round of golf together. He even paired me in the same cart with the highly respected "Dr. Crabb." I was nervous on two levels. First, I was nervous about the prospect of four and a half hours of discussion with Larry Crabb. I hoped I could keep up with him. His books (most of which I have read) are all biblically rich, thought-provoking, and probe the heart at a level many people find unnerving. I felt like a high school freshman who had been asked to attend the varsity practice only to be paired with the best athlete: excitement and apprehension bundled together. This led to my second level of nervousness: I wanted to play golf well that day. Men are men, and most men warm up to each other through shared hobbies and interests. Cars, sports, microbreweries, action movies, even golf. I knew Larry loved golf, and I wanted to make a good first impression.

First hole. First tee box. I was last to hit. I addressed the ball and went through my usual self-talk. *Head down, left arm straight,*

13

nice easy swing. To this day I have no idea what happened. But the ball didn't go more than three feet. It was one of the worst first shots I have ever hit. I looked at Larry and the other two men and said, "I actually prayed to the Lord this morning that this wouldn't happen!" They responded with a compassionate, if not awkward, laugh. As I got in the cart with Larry I thought, *So much for first impressions.*

Larry told me later, years later, that he loved what happened on that first tee. He loved the failure. He loved the comment about unanswered prayer. He loved the authenticity of coming clean with my desires and fears. He even loved the slight mortification I felt when my ball went only a few feet. Larry loves these things. He loves them not because he takes joy in other people's difficulties but because he sees God most clearly in other people's brokenness. He experiences God most acutely in his own brokenness.

This book is about what you and I do with God in the midst of our brokenness—when God doesn't make sense. How should we view Him? How should we approach Him? There are a number of options before us. We can turn on spiritual autopilot, coast awhile, and effectively place God on the back burner. Many well-meaning people do this today. Another option is that we can alter our view of God to better fit our messed-up lives. We can try to force-fit God into a paradigm that will help us make sense of our pain. This, too, is a common pathway taken by many good-hearted followers of God. It's an important question to wrestle with: What do we do with God when He seems to make no sense?

Larry has an answer: tremble and trust. These are not words I usually associate together. In my understanding, I either tremble *or* trust. I either have fear or faith. I either get bogged down in life's difficulties or I rise up and believe. I don't usually tremble *and* trust. However, this is precisely what Larry asserts. We must learn to apply soul-quaking humility with heart-abandoning faith if we are ever going to experience God as we long to.

The path this book will take us on will not be an easy one. Asking difficult, risky questions about God that many of us avoid, while simultaneously plumbing biblical depths that will challenge us to see God in a new and different light—this journey is not for the fainthearted. It's for those who join the original goldminers of the 1800s in yelling, "There's gold in them thar hills!" As those miners charged the hills, they knew the journey would not be easy. In pursuit of possible gold, however, charge on they did. This book is the gold worth pursuing in the hills.

I have personally experienced profound life change as the result of learning from Larry Crabb. I have been able to experience God in the midst of my brokenness. I'm still a pretty bad golfer, but I'm a much better man of God, husband, father, friend, and pastor.

Jamie Rasmussen
Scottsdale, Arizona

Introduction

God's Way of Thinking Doesn't Easily Fit into Our Minds

The gospel changes everything. But most of us don't quite believe it yet. It's too radical. For some it's too radical to even think it might be true. For others, it's so offensive to the deep-seated pride lodged in everyone's heart that they find it hard to accept.

We have yet to fully see gospel beauty, the beauty of pure love seen perfectly only in God, a beauty that can neither be recognized nor properly valued until our self-centered, confused minds are sufficiently humbled and opened to think like God and to trust His ways.

Life isn't going according to plan. Our story is off-script. A stack of unexpected bills, new health concerns, a for-sale house that won't sell, troubling marital tensions, an uncontrollable sexual urge that brings hidden shame, a level of listlessness bordering on depression: it's always something. Nothing is ever exactly as we want it to be, at least not for long.

17

Advice columnists tell us to deal with it as responsibly as we can and move on with life. Perhaps schedule time with a counselor or life coach. Don't focus on what's wrong. Be grateful for whatever is right. Give yourself a break; do something you enjoy. You'll feel better.

Christians understand that we need to manage whatever can be managed as best we can, with whatever help we need. But we believe in a good and loving and powerful God. So we turn to Him. We pray over whatever is troubling us. When the concerns are deeply disturbing, we get serious about prayer. We drop to our knees and pray fervently and faithfully, and we make our prayer requests known to friends, sometimes communicating with them through a prayer chain.

Nothing happens. Nothing changes. We hear no clear word from God. We see no evidence of divine intervention on our behalf. Past prayers sometimes have been answered. Why not now?

We're not deists. We believe in a caring, present God. But we wonder. Is God listening? Have we offended Him? Must we clean up our lives before He'll answer? But God is gracious. He's a patient, forgiving God. Isn't He supposed to do something? Isn't that what love does?

Difficulties continue. New ones develop. I just read an email from a friend: breast cancer. Big problems. Little problems. But always problems. We're Christians, God's loved children. We can trust Him. *To do what?*

Consider these brief vignettes of real people talking to themselves.

God wouldn't want me to put up with my husband. The man doesn't even know I exist. I feel like a nobody. God loves me too much to ever want me to hurt like this. So, with His blessing, I intend to make whatever arrangements I must to feel better about myself and to have a satisfying relationship with another man, not the one I'm stuck with now.

Our mission desperately needs funds to repair our falling-apart facility for burned-out missionaries to come and rest for a while.

If we don't receive what we need, we'll have to close down our ministry. We know we're doing God's work. We're doing what He called us to do. Surely He'll supply the necessary money.

I've been living as a single woman for decades. It really hurts that no man has pursued me. But I'm trusting God to help me get on with my life. Even though I'm still single, with no prospects for marriage in sight, I've rededicated myself to follow Jesus however, wherever, and whenever He leads. But I've just felt a lump in my breast. I just can't believe that a loving God would not answer my prayer that it be benign so I can get on with following Him on these new paths.

Every ministry door I've knocked on has remained shut. I've been to seminary. I won the preaching award my senior year. And my professors told me I had a pastor's heart. I've applied to a dozen churches that had an advertised spot for a lead or associate pastor. Nothing opened up. I'm discouraged. But I know God loves me. I'm confident I'll get the chance to pastor and preach. Would a loving God provide less?

What was the prophet Isaiah saying to us when, speaking for God, he wrote: "'My thoughts are nothing like your thoughts,' says the LORD. 'And my ways are far beyond anything you could imagine'" (Isa. 55:8)? And then, to emphasize the point he doesn't want us to miss, Isaiah adds, "For just as the heavens are higher than the earth, so my ways are higher than your ways and my thoughts higher than your thoughts" (v. 9).

Here's Isaiah's point: our thoughts and ways about how life should unfold for Jesus-followers are so much lower in wisdom than God's thoughts and ways that we sometimes cannot understand how God is going about telling His love story. So much goes wrong in so many of our lives, and it all happens on God's watch. Listen to the heart attitude of so many Christians today:

19

not ours

---

*I'm doing my best to follow God's principles for living,
to keep troubles at bay and to bring good things close,
but it's not happening. Am I really as far off-base in my
understanding of how God works as Isaiah seems to think?*

Paul echoes Isaiah with these words: "How impossible it is for us to understand his decisions and his ways! For who can know the LORD's thoughts?" (Rom. 11:33–34).

There are questions we cannot easily answer.

Why doesn't God always honor the prayers of an abused wife by straightening out her husband?

Why doesn't God reliably come through with donations needed to keep a good ministry going?

Why doesn't God display His love for every single woman who wants to be married by introducing her to a good man who wants her, and if not that, then at least bless each one with opportunities for a fulfilling life and the good health needed to seize them?

Why doesn't God advance kingdom purposes through a godly, gifted pastor-in-waiting by arranging for a church to make him their pastor? God opens the door for lots of seminary and Bible college grads to become pastors. Why not open that door for every qualified grad who feels called to the ministry?

Isaiah speaks again: "Who could ever have told God what to do or taught him his business?" (Isa. 40:12 MSG).

When God's thoughts and ways make no sense to us, we Christians are confronted with three options.

1. *Resist and Run*

Determine to follow God when we like the direction He leads. But when we don't, when His thoughts and ways seem to be taking us away from the life we want for ourselves, then we feel justified in resisting His input and running off to do whatever better fits our ideas of a good way to live. *Like Jonah.* This option is illustrated in the life of a prophet who was enraged at God's plan.

2. *Distort and Deny*

Arrange our understanding both of how God thinks about our lives and of how He lovingly moves into them so that it matches our perception of how a loving God should think and move. Deny Scripture that contradicts what we want to believe about God. Revise our theology of God's good news into principles for living that make obedience to God comfortable—comfortable obedience that we assume will bring satisfying blessings into our lives. *Like Saul.* Before Saul became Paul, he distorted the Old Testament's message into what he wanted it to say and denied the value of passages that contradicted his distortion.

3. *Tremble and Trust*

Sit under the Bible. Hear whatever God is saying. When we realize that God's way of running the world and guiding our lives makes no sense, *tremble*. Tremble before a God whose thoughts and ways are far above our thoughts and ways about what the truly good life is and how to live it. Feel our confusion. Own our doubts. Embrace our fears. Face our disappointment. Experience our anguish.

Then *trust*. Trust the Judge of the earth to do right, to always advance purposes we will one day gladly agree were good. Accept that no one can fully unravel the mystery of prayer. Choose to live by faith in God's goodness, to deny authority to what our dim eyes can see. With the eyes of faith, gaze on the unfolding story of God that with the eyes of sight we may not recognize as a story of love. Humble ourselves. Confess our pride. We think we know more than we do.

Tremble before the incomprehensible God and trust that He is good. Trust that His love is committed to our growing awareness of the deepest and happiest well-being that's available to us now, that His love will lead us into an eternity where we will know every delight we were created to enjoy. Gaze on the cross. Remember Christ's death. Nowhere is the love of the incomprehensible God more fully and clearly displayed.

But always remember: tastes now, the full banquet later. Tremble before what our eyes can see and our hearts can feel. Trust in what our faith can believe, that the longed-for satisfaction of our deepest thirst lies ahead. *Like Habakkuk.* Habakkuk's story illustrates what it looks like to respond well when God's ways make no sense.

We know Jonah was wrong. The youngest Christian intuitively knows it's never right to resist God, even when His thoughts about what makes life good and His ways of arranging for life to be good make no sense to us. Jonah's resistance was flagrant. When God's instructions enraged him, Jonah wouldn't even speak to God. He refused to accept God's plan for his life.

Our ways of resisting tend to be a bit more subtle. Fervent prayers that go unanswered seem to justify a righteous-feeling sulk. "I prayed my wife's cancer would be healed. And now she's dead."

But perhaps the most insidious form of resistance among today's Christians is to selectively ignore biblical data in order to embrace a comfortable and convenient understanding of how God thinks and works. A well-known Christian leader was once asked to share his secret of parenting. All three of his then-adult children were leading exemplary lives: successful, moral, and godly. "From the day we knew we were pregnant, my wife and I were on our knees every night, holding hands and praying for God's blessing on each child," he said.

With his wife, a good friend has prayed fervently and continuously for his four children. One is a Christian. Three are not. Two have spent time in jail. Perhaps they didn't pray together on their knees. Is that the formula for answered prayer? Shaping God into who we want Him to be, believing in a God of love whose divine power can be managed, is a common way to resist the God of sovereign, holy love whose thoughts and ways are not subject to our control.

In whatever form, resisting God often leads to running away from Him. But not always. Moses was not excited about God's call for him to return to Egypt to lead His people out of bondage. Jeremiah shrunk back from God's summons to deliver a difficult message to Judah. But their resistance had more to do with fearful hesitation than proud defiance. Neither man ran away from God. Jonah did, as far away as a ship could take him.

However motivated, our version of running away from God too often allows us to believe we're still tracking with Him. While declaring our allegiance to Jesus, we betray His authority over us by reshaping God's way of leading us into directions we can easily follow. Saul, who later became the apostle Paul, illustrates that pattern. We'll see that pattern in chapter 3. The Golden Calf Syndrome is still with us today, reducing God to a deity whose thoughts and ways our flesh can enjoy.

When the Israelites got impatient with Moses for remaining so long on Mount Sinai, Aaron yielded to their grumbling by gathering their gold and making a "golden calf" (Exod. 32:4 ESV). When the God of Moses failed to serve the people as they wanted, they came up with a more cooperative god to serve.

None of us is safe from worshiping this golden calf, our designer god. We confess that it would be wrong to run away from God when the path He wants us to take seems to be leading toward hard times. But perhaps we've misunderstood His directions. Better to come up with a set of biblical principles, what we can think of as moral choices, that, if followed, will move God to give us what we want.

23

And what we want are legitimate goods that we assume God wants for us as well: good family, good friends, good job, good income, good ministry, and good health. When God grants these blessings, and sometimes He does, of course we should gratefully enjoy them. To do otherwise would be wrong.

But recognize the problem. We've distorted God's story into a system, a formula for satisfying us, with little thought given to what would glorify God, to how we could love and relate in ways that would reveal His nature of suffering love to others. In G. K. Chesterton's way of putting it, we've become chess players, not poets.[1] We make the right moves on the chess board of life, and God responds by letting us win the match. Pray on your knees every day, and God will work (sovereignly?) to provide the kids we want. Get it right and life will work. That's today's gospel, for now, in this life. And when we die, heaven forever. Could there be better news?

Preaching the false gospel can build churches. Writing about it can sell books. But this message is a modern version of the "other" gospel Paul warned us about:

> I am shocked that you are turning away so soon from God. . . . You are following a different way that pretends to be the Good News but is not the Good News at all. You are being fooled by those who deliberately twist the truth concerning Christ. (Gal. 1:6–7)

Today's twisted version of a false gospel perverts the truth that God is love into the lie that God is cooperative. I wonder: If we sincerely prayed David's prayer—"Search me, O God, and know my heart. . . . Point out anything in me that offends you" (Ps. 139:23–24)—would more of us realize that we've actually bought into this lie? God's love compels Him to cooperate with the plan He's come up with. In our thinking, that plan is obvious, simple, and fair. *If I do well, He'll see to it that my life goes well.* That's the lie. That's not God's plan. When we believe it, and life does go well, we feel proud, justly rewarded for our good behavior. If life does not go well, even though we've lived well, we become disillusioned and disappointed with God.

Growing up in a Christian home in the late forties and fifties, I sang hymns and choruses in church and youth conferences that primed me to embrace a false gospel. Here's one example: "Count your many blessings, name them one by one, and it will surprise you what the Lord hath done."[2] No one can count blessings that God has not provided, so as a child I assumed that the God who loves me would pour out blessings for me to excitedly count. Call that the Scrooge McDuck Syndrome. Remember the cartoon character who sat in his treasure room counting and recounting all his money? The author of that hymn may have had *spiritual* blessings in *heavenly* places in mind for me to count, but each time I sang those words I felt gratefully justified in trusting God to always surprise me with more blessings of the *earthly* variety.

Another familiar old hymn comes to mind: "'Tis so sweet to trust in Jesus, and to take him at his word."[3] *Sweet* wasn't a commonly used word in a cool teenage boy's vocabulary, but I knew what it meant. In my thinking, this hymn was encouraging me to trust Jesus for the blessings that would make me happy. And if I was to take Him at His word, I could of course assume that Jesus had promised to make my life a sweet adventure: minimum troubles, maximum blessings. The promise I thought God had made had little to do with the happy privilege, undeserved but guaranteed, of *relating* with God; I imagined it had everything to do with the assumed right, deserved and guaranteed, to *use* God, to expect the good things in life I badly wanted, things that a loving God would generously provide. Shouldn't He?

One more chorus (there are plenty of others): "Every day with Jesus is sweeter than the day before."[4] Believe the false gospel, and you'll expect pleasant days ahead. But for some life may soon teach you to sing, "Every day with Jesus is harder than the day before."

25

During my growing-up years, the "truth" of that chorus—would my church's leaders ever let us sing untrue choruses?—prompted me to assume that if life were going well today, I could only imagine the good things tomorrow would bring. And if somehow a bad day interfered with my expectations, I could trust Jesus for a better day tomorrow.

No one needs to know those songs to arrive at the notion that if there really is a loving God, we can depend on Him to give good things to good people, like us.

We've all come up with an understanding of how God thinks and acts that fits comfortably with our understanding of how a loving God should think and act.

The older I get, the more it seems, though not by design, that my books become autobiographical. Now in my seventies, I find myself trembling, more than ever, before a God I cannot understand. I'm aware of new levels of confusion that won't yield to clarity, of repeated failures I can't seem to control, of a more intense thirst that longs for gulps of living water when all that seems to be available are sips.

Few days pass without my realizing that I'm yet again at a familiar crossroads. One of three paths must be chosen. One, I resist God, taking a path I believe will offer satisfaction that won't be mine to enjoy if I follow God. Two, I distort what I hear from God into thoughts about what makes life good and into ways of arranging for the good life I want, proudly assuming that my distortions are God-honoring interpretations of Scripture justified by thinking God's love is more indulgent than demanding. Or three, I tremble in the presence of mystery and trust that God is advancing the plot of an unimaginably good love story.

The choice, a daily choice, is mine to make. I'm hoping that what I have to say in this book will encourage both reader and author to know that the right choice, the only choice that leads to the joy that every human soul most wants, is to tremble and trust. Then together we'll be able to count the blessings that lead us to life as God defines it. We'll know it actually is sweet to follow Jesus, and that every day can draw us closer into relationship with Him and form us to relate more like He relates. Then we'll increasingly put divine love on display in all our relationships. And doing so will surprise us with joy—with a different, better kind of happiness that earthbound blessings can never provide.

---〜---

PART 1

When God's Ways Make No Sense, What Then?

Three Stories, Three Answers

More often now than earlier in my Christian life, I find myself asking three rather weighty questions, questions that fifty years of counseling have convinced me that many others are asking as well. Perhaps not out loud. The questions might be heard as evidence of little faith, maybe as questions that really shouldn't be asked by Christians who trust Jesus to guide them through their lives.

But these are three questions that life will at some point nudge every honest Christian to ask.

Question 1: *Why Must Suffering Play Such a Big Role in the Christian Life?*

Shouldn't a loving God protect us better than He does? Why does He disappoint us so often by doing nothing in response to some pretty important prayer requests? Life hurts, and God allows the source of our pain to remain. Why? We know suffering has its good purposes. Nothing else so effectively can expose a demanding spirit ("I'm entitled to better treatment!") and prompt much-needed repentance. And the suffering of prolonged uncertainty over health issues and financial difficulties encourages deepened dependence on the God who is in control of tomorrow.

But can't a serious Christian mature just as well in good times? Couldn't whatever suffering that may be necessary for our spiritual formation be less severe and more quickly ended? Must so many go through so much? *It doesn't make sense.*

Question 2: *Why Must Failure Be Such an Ongoing Part of the Christian Life?*

Paul saw himself as a wretched man, not before he was miraculously converted but afterward, when he was a seasoned, unusually mature follower of Jesus. In Romans 7:24, the Greek word Paul chose that we translate "wretched" (ESV) clearly implies that the great apostle continued to bear the weight of the enduring misery of human weakness. In his words, "I want to do what is right, but I can't" (v. 18). So much for a sugarcoated understanding of a changed life. Paul was never free from sin—from sin's penalty, yes, but not from sinning. Like all Christians today, Paul was not a slave to sin. The sin nature is no longer a master that Christians involuntarily obey. Until heaven, though, Christians struggle with sin's appeal and too often yield.

30

Earlier in that same chapter, Paul told us that thanks to the gospel we can now live in the "new way of living in the Spirit" (v. 6). Does that mean it is possible for a Christian to harness the Spirit's power so that recurring sin will no longer be a problem in life? As an old man, the apostle John looked back on his life and warned everyone that "If we claim we have no sin, we are only fooling ourselves and not living in the truth" (1 John 1:8). It seems God leads us *through* failure toward maturity, rather than doing whatever is needed for us to *move past* ongoing failure. What does gospel power mean in a Christian's life? Shouldn't it mean that when we want to do right, we reliably can? Apparently not! But why not? *It doesn't make sense.*

The two questions require a third.

Question 3: *How Are We to Respond to Seemingly Random Suffering with No Obvious Purpose and to Repeated Failure That We Try Hard to Resist but Sometimes Can't?*

I might have preferred to respond to the first two questions with easy-to-follow counsel. I could have written a book suggesting how Christians can routinely experience the presence of God with an intensity that reduces suffering into a short-lived anomaly in an otherwise happily blessed life. Perhaps the faithful practice of spiritual disciplines and contemplative prayer, both important ingredients in a Christian's journey, would deliver pain-eclipsing joy into our lives. But a Christian journey is one that follows Christ, the man of sorrows who knew joy *in the middle of pain.*

Or I could highlight the requirement of obedience to Christ's commands, and speak of the Spirit's power that enables us to live without significant failure. But Scripture insists, and experience confirms, that we will suffer and sin. Hardship and failure (the latter more easily denied) are part of every Christian's life. In line with the apostle John's teaching about "fooling ourselves" and his own experience, Martin Luther wrote in his first thesis, "When our Lord and Master Jesus Christ said 'Repent,' he intended that the entire life of believers should be repentance."[1]

This third question must be asked by every Christian who wrestles with the first two, and it deserves a thoughtfully biblical response. That necessity prompted me to write this book.

1

A Christian's Response to an Incomprehensible God

Three Options

[Am I following the Lord? Or am I asking Him to follow me?] ⚘
Maybe I'm in danger of becoming a modern-day Jonah, feeling
so disappointed and angry over God's way of directing my life
that I drop any pretense of being a God-follower.

Fifty years ago I began my doctoral program in clinical psychology.
Before arriving on campus at the University of Illinois, I made
a private decision to abandon Christianity. God wasn't doing in me
what I knew needed to be done. I had rededicated my life to Christ
a dozen times during my teenage years and was still struggling with
unabated lust, insecurity, jealousy, and personal ambition that had
more to do with my dreams than God's plan. Christianity as I knew
it, and I was an orthodox evangelical, had failed me. I decided to
give psychology a chance to help me figure out what was wrong and
change me.

The adventure didn't work out so well. Five years later I wore doctoral robes that were draped over a still lustful, insecure, jealous, and personally ambitious young man. I moved back to Christianity, convinced there was hope nowhere else. Five decades later I'm still wondering why God allows so much struggle in people's lives and why He doesn't arrange for failure to be a distant memory in the lives of His followers.

It's hard to dismiss the thought: There must be a way—more fervent prayer? increased passion for ministry? faithful practice of spiritual disciplines?—to arrange for my senior years to be golden, with less struggle and more victory. Am I trying to maneuver God to bless me in ways I imagine a loving God would want to bless a man who has been following Him for more than sixty years now? Could I be worshiping a golden calf in my "Christian" efforts to arrange for golden years?

What are God's thoughts on the matter? Does He see things differently? What are His ways of loving me that I can count on? Am I open to hearing Him tell me what His thoughts and ways actually are? And the big question: *How will I respond if I do hear from God?* Am I in danger of responding like Saul?

When Jonah heard from God, he resisted and ran. (I tell his story in the next chapter.) Before he became Paul, Saul heard God speak through a serious study of the Old Testament. But he distorted what he heard to fit what better suited his understanding of religion. And he denied the meaning of every passage that led him to a different way of thinking. The Messiah a slaughtered lamb? Jews and Gentiles becoming one family of God? Unthinkable! (We'll look at Saul's story in chapter 3.)

Remember Habakkuk? (I review his story in chapter 4.) He heard something from God that he really did not like. Evil Babylon would punish less evil Judah? That made no sense. But Habakkuk did not resist and run. He did not distort what he heard from God into a more pleasing message; he did not deny the unpleasant truth that

God told him. Instead, he trembled in confusion and fear, then trusted God to always be telling a good story, even when the story ran into some really hard chapters. Habakkuk is a model for Christians today.

I remember as a thirty-year-old enjoying lunch with eighty-year-old Dr. William Hendriksen, a renowned New Testament scholar. I had just read his commentary on Galatians and was eager to hear his take on the "other" gospel Paul was warning us to reject. For more than an hour that seemed like twenty minutes, I listened to this brilliant professor answer what to him must have been simple questions.

But then he surprised me. As our time drew to a close, Dr. Hendriksen reached across the table, rested his age-marked hand on my arm, and with moist eyes said, "Oh, Brother Larry, I think I'm just beginning to understand the gospel."

At the very real risk of including myself in company where I don't belong, now in my early seventies I'm thinking that perhaps I'm just beginning to understand the gospel. It's so much more but never less than forgiveness of sin, restored relationship with God, and the promise of heaven forever. It's a call to radical discipleship, to a life of perseverance through unpredictable suffering and of joy in knowing there is no condemnation for ongoing failure. It is not an easy life. It wasn't meant to be.

Think of it this way:

- If I hear from God and feel no urge to resist and run, thinking that He's asking too much, I haven't heard from God. My view of the gospel is shallow.
- If I hear from God and am not tempted to distort what I hear into a call to a comfortable life, and if I'm not inclined to deny any real attention to passages that say otherwise, I haven't heard from God. I'm believing another gospel.
- If I hear from God and see no reason to tremble at the cost required to trust God no matter what struggles come my way

and what ongoing sin continues, I have not heard from God. I've heard a cheap gospel.

When Christians, properly settled on the plan of salvation in Christ, hear the call of God on their lives, something deep in their souls is disrupted. When Christians hear God's call, not simply to a specific ministry or to a moral lifestyle or to theological study but to become a certain kind of person no one can ever fully become this side of heaven, a battle begins. The journey finds its way onto a narrow road.

It is then we quietly expect God to make the journey easier by doing at least two things: one, to bless us with enough good things and fulfilling opportunities to make the journey appealing; and two, to supply the power needed for us to overcome both our addictive sins and our relational sins and to overwhelm our weakness with the Spirit's strength so that sinful failure becomes only an occasional concern.

God does neither, not routinely. But why not? God loves us; He is good and He is powerful. The Father is in control over all that happens. The Son is praying for us as a faithful high priest. And the Spirit has moved into our souls, stirring the divine energy now alive in our new hearts. Suffering should diminish. Things should more often go our way. Prayers should be answered. And sin should become less of a problem, perhaps only an occasional slip now and then. Victory in Christ, victory over former temptations, a victorious Christian life—it all should be ours to celebrate and enjoy. That's how many of us think.

When difficulties intrude and failure continues, *we meet the incomprehensible God*. Who is He? What is He up to? We hear the gospel plan for our lives, a plan that includes trouble, hard times, failure, and ongoing sin, and it's not what we had in mind. *It doesn't make sense*. What then?

Three options present themselves. I listed them in the introduction. In more concise form, let me describe them again. It will prove helpful to keep these three options in mind as you keep reading.

Option 1: Resist God's call to a life of difficulty and ongoing failure and run from Him toward a way of living that seems better. Live for prosperity and healing, or at least for relief. You'll feel better.

Option 2: Stick with God but distort His message to better line up with your thoughts about what life should be and with your ways of understanding how God should lead you. In the process, convince yourself you're still following God.

Option 3: Hear the gospel story that will lead you through suffering and failure to hope only in Christ, never in yourself. Tremble before the God whose thoughts and ways, so far above yours, will at times make no sense to you. But trust that the God who died for you when you deserved eternal judgment is up to something good. He is always telling a good story. He can never do less.

The story of Jonah illustrates option 1. As we look at his story in the next chapter, we might see a little bit of Jonah in ourselves.

2

Resist and Run
(When Doing Wrong Feels Right)

The Story of Jonah

When fervent prayers go unanswered, when a second shoe drops and a third one follows, when all sense of God's loving involvement in our lives vanishes, then like Jonah, we may be tempted to resist God, run from Him, and manage life as best we can.

I have studied the book of Jonah for many hours over many years. Many times I have taught what I then understood, in some degree correctly, to be God's message imbedded in Jonah's story. But like anyone with even a modicum of humble wisdom, I never assumed I had heard everything God wanted me to hear in that short book, or in any other book of the Bible. There's always more.

Every thoughtful Bible student, whether an academically trained scholar or, like me, a self-studying learner, keeps in mind that all sixty-six love letters in the divine correspondence were written by an infinite author with no limits to His wisdom. He is the God whose thoughts and ways will always prove to be beyond ours and will often make little or no sense to our limited, finite, and still-fallen minds.

But it's true that this transcendent God delights to continually share more slivers of His wisdom with us. When reading the Bible, we therefore have good reason to approach our study eagerly anticipating those providentially arranged moments when God's Spirit leads us in directions we never thought to travel before. When those moments come, our subsequent teaching opportunities, whether spoken or written, will go over old ground with new passion or introduce new ideas that build on old ground.

A New Question

In preparation for writing this chapter, I reread, restudied, and re-reflected on Jonah's story, written either by the prophet, who hopefully learned his lesson, or by someone with whom he later shared his strange story. Either way, we can be confident that God's Spirit hovered over the writer to make certain that what He was saying could be heard by people with open ears for generations to come.

This time through the text, a question came to mind I had never before thought to ask. The question intrigued me. It may be old to you. It was new to me. And asking it let me see something in the story I had not focused on before. Could it be that I'm just beginning to understand what God wants me to hear in this one-of-a-kind narrative?

The question is this: Was God more lovingly committed to providing Nineveh's repentance or to forming Jonah's soul?

The obvious answer, which is obviously right, is *both*. God's good heart was on display in His call to Jonah to travel to Nineveh and in His ongoing dealings with His reluctant prophet. But notice something else, something that is obvious but easily overlooked in its possible significance. Jonah's preaching to Nineveh and the city's repentance are both recorded in one chapter, but three chapters are devoted to revealing how God worked to form Jonah's soul. That may be suggestive.

Suggestive of what? Perhaps this: in God's thinking about what matters most and in His way of carrying out His thought, ministry (as we commonly understand the term to mean doing something for someone else) is vital. But ministry loses life-changing power when it flows from a soul not committed to ongoing formation. Soul formation in individual persons is essential for deep work in others. That thought leads to another: *missional work is designed to be the overflowing of formational work.* Ministry to others gains power as the Spirit ministers His soul-forming work in us.

Forming Christians do better kingdom work. It happens, of course, that some level of ministry is accomplished by Christians who are not especially interested in personal soul work. Good things, impressive to our sensationalist culture, develop through zealous Christians on the mission field and through gifted Christians behind pulpits, Christians who are too busy for the slow work of formation and, given their apparent success, see little need for it.

But until Christ returns to make everything new, including people, culture, and currently weed-filled gardens, God is now devoting Himself to one principal project: *forming followers of Jesus into lovers like Jesus.* In speaking to the Galatians, Paul's deepest passion was not to see their church increase in numbers, to encourage an effective conference ministry, to send more missionaries to foreign fields, or to change culture in God-honoring ways; it was to see Christ fully formed in their lives. Of course Jonah's ministry to Nineveh mattered to God. But one gets the impression that the formation of Jonah's soul is the focus in this story.

Today's Christian culture has largely reversed those priorities. Youth pastors, for example, are often held more accountable for doubling the size of their youth group than for opening their own souls to the Spirit's shaping work. Have we forgotten that forming pastors are best equipped to do forming ministry? Leaders and laypeople alike too often devote more resources to ministry size, ministry support, and measurable ministry effectiveness than to formational ministry in themselves. It's important to notice that sizable, funded, culturally successful ministry does not require ministers to examine their souls. In a Christian culture addicted to visible success in ministry, little to no effort is expended to discern whether the motivation for ministry has more to do with glorifying God through kingdom advancement or with ego enhancement through job results and security.

If we're to live together in a kind of relationally loving community that requires the Spirit's deep and ongoing work in our individual souls, we must not only assign priority to soul formation over ministry activities but also understand that soul formation is relational formation. And nowhere is relational formation, learning to love like Jesus, more clearly and powerfully displayed than in one-on-one, soul-to-soul conversations. Jonah could prophesy. He could preach. But could he relate?

Why do I ask? *Because nowhere is divine love more severely compromised by unseen and unconfessed self-serving motives than in conversations.* We have no record that Jonah searched his heart and owned motives that required repentance. Jonah was wrong. Unlike Jonah, I realize I am to search my heart.

When I'm talking with people, am I protecting my interests or serving the interests of others? Am I relating to receive something from another or to release something in me for the good of another? Am I ruled by a felt inadequacy to an unrecognized extent that impels me to display my value, or am I ruled by the Spirit's adequacy that frees me to display the value of Christ by how I relate?

Spirit-guided self-examination, which neither Jonah nor many of us today know much about, reveals both the ugliness of self-serving passion that warrants repentance and the beauty of divine love that can then be released through repentance.

Too often in today's Christian culture, ministry is centered in promoting external change, such as church growth, increased giving, better-attended programs, and additional mission projects. When such ministry is valued over formation, self-examination resulting in repentance of relational sin is undervalued. When formation is valued before (and during) externally focused ministry, self-examination is recognized as crucial. And pouring oneself out for the spiritual formation of others is understood to be ministry just as much as promoting external changes is. From the record we have of Jonah's dialogue with God, it seems abundantly clear that he was aware of nothing in the interior world of his soul that would lead him toward humble brokenness, and of nothing in his thoughts and motives that required repentance. Neither did Jonah glimpse into his soul with hope in God that brought recognition of a deep, joyful thirst to put God's heart on display as he preached to Nineveh. Therefore, he never fell in line with God's loving will and, as a result, never prayed for Nineveh's repentance.

Something in the way Jonah was thinking made it seem reasonable to him to resist God and run from Him when His ways made no sense to Jonah. As a man not yet on the journey of spiritual formation, Jonah cared only about himself and his comfortable life in Israel as a well-received prophet. Look with me now as I briefly highlight five key elements in Jonah's story that let us see what Jonah was thinking. We might just recognize similar thinking in ourselves that makes it seem reasonable for us to resist and run when God's thoughts and ways are counter to ours.

Five Key Elements in Jonah's Story

One: *Jonah is the only prophet whose story is told in the Bible who wouldn't even speak to God when God's ways made no sense to him.*

Remember the text. God said, "Get up and go to the great city of Nineveh." Then, without a word, "Jonah got up and went in the opposite direction to get away from the LORD" (Jon. 1:2–3). Without first registering his concerns with God, Jonah resisted God and ran away from Him. Why?

The answer comes to us through Jonah's earlier history. He had been called by God once before to prophesy. Things were bad in Israel. Land had been lost. The economy was in shambles. God "saw the bitter suffering of everyone in Israel, and that there was no one in Israel, slave or free, to help them" (2 Kings 14:26).

It was then that God called Jonah to deliver a message that made sense to His prophet: tell King Jeroboam II that lost land will be recovered, the economy will turn around, and life in Israel will improve (see 2 Kings 14:25). God said it would happen. It did. No doubt Jonah's popularity as God's prophet soared. During that time two other prophets, Hosea and Amos, were also instructed by God to speak to Israel. But their message was different. These two men strongly denounced Israel's sinfulness and made it clear that God's people deserved judgment, not blessing. Little imagination is required to decide which of the three prophets was best received.

Israel did prosper. Only one clear danger remained: Assyria. Nineveh was its capital. Known for its eagerness to expand its boundaries and to cruelly subjugate conquered citizens, Assyria loomed as a constant threat to Israel's continued good fortune. One could assume that Israel's God, who loved His people and was all-powerful, would take whatever steps were necessary to keep Israel secure. One step was obvious: destroy Nineveh. That made sense.

I can picture the self-satisfied King Jeroboam leading a rally of Israelites chanting, "Destroy Nineveh!" And I can see Jonah in the front of the crowd, smiling his approval and trusting God to be listening and planning to take action. But then Jonah suddenly sensed that God was about to speak to him. He went to a quiet place to listen. Surely the same God who had told Jonah to prophesy prosperity for Israel would now prophesy destruction to Nineveh. What else would a loving God do?

Jonah listened. God spoke: *Go to Nineveh. Give them a chance to repent. I do not want to destroy them.* To himself, Jonah muttered, "I knew God was compassionate and merciful. But I never dreamed He would show His kindness to an enemy of Israel. I just told Israel things would go well for them. Now I'm to say that our worst enemy will remain a threat to our good times? It doesn't make any sense."

A woman I know felt clearly led by God to marry the man who courted her. During the wedding ceremony, together they publicly declared their intent to serve God in foreign missions. The couple beamed with joy. Pastor, parents, siblings, and friends all shared their God-based happiness. Three years later, after two years of fruitful missionary work, the man told his wife he was attracted to other men. He insisted they return home. He then filed for divorce, surrendered custody of their infant son, and quickly married a former male lover.

Her words to me: "Why would God let me marry a man who He knew would break my heart? It makes no sense." Her husband clearly resisted God's will and ran from God, but the same option became appealing to his betrayed wife.

It's the story of many. When God's blessings are taken away on God's watch, the urge rises up: resist God's further leading. He is not worthy of trust. Run away from His plan toward a better life than the one God seems willing to provide. When God's ways make no sense, resist and run. *That* makes sense.

Two: *Jonah had no interest in sharing his struggle with a God who made no sense. So he boarded a ship to get far away from God and, once on board, fell fast asleep.*

Jonah resisted God. He wouldn't bring his concerns to Him. And he ran away from God. He booked passage on a ship bound for Tarshish. In so doing, he effectively resigned his role as God's prophet. His insides must have been swirling with anger, confusion, and fear. Not wanting to deal with the turmoil churning in his soul, Jonah boarded the ship, perhaps greeted the sailors, then quickly climbed down into the ship's hold and fell asleep. Easier to sleep than to face troubling thoughts and emotions. The pattern continues today. Two illustrations make the point:

- A friend of mine was married to his worst critic. "Nothing I do ever pleases her." God's call to love his wife made no sense to him. "The more I'm nice to her, the more she thinks I fail her." So he "fell asleep" in workaholism and golf, arranging to be away from home as much as he could. It made life easier. And the satisfaction he felt in career success and a low golf handicap kept him from feeling guilt both over resisting God's call to love his wife and over running away from God into a plan for his life that made more sense than God's.

- A woman was blessed with the good things of life: good husband, good kids, good money, good health, good friends, good ministry as a Bible study leader, and good looks. But one early morning she couldn't sleep. She sensed that God was calling her to examine the quality of her relating with family and friends. Was she pouring divine love into others, or was she simply enjoying her blessings? The call unnerved her. She "fell asleep" in her blessings, more soundly than before, keeping her distance from a God who was calling her to something more than a comfortably blessed life.

Three: *Jonah's belly-of-the-fish repentance was shallow, and therefore had no power to form his soul. He never confessed the sin of resisting God and running away from Him.*

Notice the following:

- Jonah cried out to the Lord in his "great trouble" (Jon. 2:1–2), not in his great sin.

big difference

- Jonah told God that He had thrown him "into the ocean depths" (v. 3). But had Jonah truly repented of sin, I assume the storm would have stopped, the sailors would have turned the ship around and returned Jonah to Joppa, and he would have gone on his God-appointed mission to Nineveh with a clean heart. God did not throw Jonah into the ocean. Jonah threw himself. *wow!, and God's mercy saved him!*

- Jonah complained, "O LORD, you have driven me from your presence" (v. 4). No, Jonah ran away from God's presence. He boarded a ship "hoping to escape from the LORD by sailing to Tarshish" (1:3). Who wouldn't run away from such an unreasonable God who would withhold all sense of His presence when someone most needed to experience it? Jonah's resistance was God's fault. Or so Jonah apparently thought.

- Jonah offered "earnest prayer" to God (2:7). To mercifully use him as God's prophet to Nineveh? Or to rescue him from trouble? *When was his earnest prayer? For himself*

- Jonah scorned pagans who "worship false gods" (v. 8), then referred to himself as a better person, one who would worship God "with songs of praise" (v. 9). Praise to a God who would bless his ministry to Nineveh? Or praise to a God who would deliver him from the stinking prison of a fish's belly?

God could not honor Jonah's feeble effort at repentance. He ordered the fish to "spit Jonah out onto the beach" (v. 10). The Hebrew for "spit out" indicates getting rid of garbage. God was clearly not affirming a changed heart in Jonah. Jonah did go to Nineveh, but still at odds with God's purpose that made no sense to him.

Am I Jonah? When life becomes difficult, my "spiritual inclination" is to repent of any recognized failure—but perhaps only to get God off my back. Confession designed to restore lost blessings is a management technique. It is not repentance.

Four: *Jonah went to Nineveh and faithfully delivered God's message. He did the right thing with a wrong heart. He still wanted Nineveh destroyed.*

At a real cost to himself, Jonah did travel to Nineveh, on foot. He walked nearly nine hundred miles over rough terrain through dangerous country. Uninvited, he showed up in Nineveh and preached a message that would likely offend everybody. Beneath outward conformity to God's will, a reservoir of vile motivation may exist. It did in Jonah. It happens in Christians today:

- Men "love" their wives to avoid tension.
- Women "love" their husbands to win love in return.
- Parents "love" their children to enjoy good kids.
- Friends "love" their friends to keep a friendship.
- Pastors "love" their people to keep them coming to church and supporting their ministry.
- Missionaries "love" locals in their mission field to report ministry success in letters to supporters.

Too cynical? No, there are wonderful examples of husbands, wives, parents, friends, pastors, and missionaries who love in order to glorify God, to put the love of Jesus on display. But the danger remains alive in yet-to-be-glorified saints: we can do good to others with self-serving motives. It's an insidious version of resisting God's call to self-denial and of running away from God into self-enhancement.

Five: *Jonah's resisting and running was a response to a God he did not know.*

A brief sketch of Jonah's history makes the point:

- Jonah's father was a man named Amittai, which means "faithfulness," suggesting Jonah was raised in a God-honoring home.

It is likely that as a child Jonah embraced who we might refer to as the *family God*.

- Jonah's God-fearing father no doubt prayed to God that Israel would repent and return to true worship. It didn't happen. As a teenager, like many teens in subsequent generations, perhaps Jonah began to wonder if the *family God* was in fact an *uninvolved God*, a deistic deity.

- As an adult, Jonah saw God get involved. He heard God say to him, "I see My people's distress. Tell them things will soon get better." The *uninvolved God* suddenly turned into the *triumphalist God*, a generous God who would lead His people into blessing after blessing.

- But soon after, God told Jonah to preach to Nineveh. "I don't want to destroy that great city so full of people and animals." God didn't want to destroy Israel's most threatening enemy? In Jonah's mind, the *triumphalist God* quickly was replaced by the *incomprehensible God*, a God who made no sense. Jonah resisted and ran.

- Spit out from three days in a fish's belly, a chagrined Jonah preached to Nineveh. When Nineveh repented, God actually let the wicked city live. Unacceptable! Inexcusable! Jonah then found himself in the presence of the *intolerable God*. It would be better to die than to live in a world governed by a God whose thoughts and ways were not only incomprehensible but now intolerable. Jonah said, "O Lord, please take my life from me, for it is better for me to die than to live" (4:3 ESV).

Remember, Jonah had just been shaded from the hot sun when God arranged for the shade-providing plant to wither and die. Jonah was sorry the plant died. It wasn't right. It was then God spoke His final soul-forming words to Jonah. "You pity the plant. . . . Should I not pity Nineveh?" (vv. 10, 11 ESV). Now, here's the point: the

Hebrew word translated "pity" literally means *to have a tear in one's eye.*

God was introducing Himself to Jonah, introducing the God Jonah had never before met. I hear God saying this:

> Jonah, you once believed in the *family* God. Your faith as a child was more inherited than chosen. You then saw Me as the *uninvolved God,* unresponsive to your godly father's prayers. Later, when My call on your life made sense to you, I became the *triumphalist God,* the God who would cooperate with how you wanted your story to be told.
>
> But then My command to provide Israel's worst enemy with the opportunity to repent and live frustrated you, and I quickly became the *incomprehensible God* whose ways made no sense. It was then you felt justified in resisting Me and running away from Me. When I brought you back from your ill-advised boat trip, persuading you to go to Nineveh by arranging for you to spend three days in the belly of a fish I created for that purpose, your worst fear was realized. I chose to let Nineveh live. And now you're treating Me like the *intolerable God.*
>
> Jonah, see Me now as I most truly am: the *suffering* God. A tear wells up in My eye when I look at people I love who have turned away from Me. My love makes Me willing to pay whatever price I must to forgive them and restore them as My much-loved children. Jonah, if My suffering, sacrificing love fails to melt your cold heart and draw you to trust Me, nothing will.

To Christians today, through the story of Jonah, God is inviting us to believe that everything He does or doesn't do is an expression of His unfailing love. When we see God as He is, we will no longer resist His ways when they make no sense. We will no longer run away from Him into a "better" life than God provides. We may tremble, but we will trust. His thoughts and His ways will then be a source of never-ending delight.

But for now, until we see Jesus face-to-face, we will never fully see God as He truly is. Resisting and running will remain a temptation, a "reasonable" option when God's ways make no sense. Complete freedom from the downward pull of sin comes later. "We know that when he appears we shall be like him, because we shall see him as he is. And everyone who thus hopes in him purifies himself as he is pure" (1 John 3:2–3 ESV).

3

Distort and Deny
(The Counterfeit Gospel)

Then and Now: The Story of Saul

Before he met Jesus, Saul of Tarsus had bought into a wrong view of God's goodness. After he met Jesus, Saul (now Paul) quickly embraced a radically changed understanding of the gospel.

Is it possible that many of us today have, like Saul, come up with a mistaken understanding of God's good news? Without realizing it, are we now believing a counterfeit gospel?

Think how we come to our theological beliefs, especially our understanding of the good news God is giving us in the gospel of Christ. Everyone who believes there is a God (and that He is not the devil) agrees that in some sense He is good. We implicitly assume that we will warmly welcome whatever He wants to tell us about His plans, easily embracing the news as good. We further assume that we will cheerfully receive whatever our good, loving, and sovereign God allows in our lives as unmistakable evidence of His goodness.

But those assumptions inevitably will be sorely challenged. Bad things happen that we simply cannot call good. We shouldn't be surprised. Jesus told us to expect hard times, in some cases even a form of martyrdom. The news He brought to us from His Father, what He somehow manages to think of as good news, in our ears can sound like bad news, news we wouldn't expect to hear from a good and loving Father. To maintain confidence in God's goodness, it may seem necessary to twist God's news into something He has not said, something that we cannot accept as good news without mental gymnastics.

One possible, and I think common, twist is this: live right and God will see to it that life will turn out right. Trust Him and good things will happen. Paul did tell us that "we know that for those who love God all things work together for good, for those who are called according to his purpose" (Rom. 8:28 ESV). The "good" toward which God is working must be understood. It is not a pleasantly blessed life. Verse 29 tells us that God's purpose is to form us into the image of His Son. That is the "good" God is always working to bring about. But notice: Paul did not say that all things work together for good *for those whom God loves*. Had he put it that way, I could rest more easily in God's sovereign plans for my life. God loves everyone, so deeply that He doesn't wish "that any should perish" (2 Pet. 3:9 ESV).

I know God loves me. But not everyone loves God. Do I? Do I even know what it means to love anyone, by God's standards? Could Paul be telling me that if my love for God doesn't measure up to the yardstick of gladly surrendering to His will, then I might have a hard time seeing how life's setbacks are working for my good?

I do know that I have been called according to His purpose. Every Christian has been rescued from eternal death, the death of utter aloneness, to advance the relational plot of the love story God is telling. But do I understand the story line? Am I committed to furthering the plot no matter what cost may be required? Perhaps I really think His purpose has more to do (or should have more to do) with blessing my life as I want it blessed than with forming my soul as the Holy Spirit wants it formed.

Good Things?

Maybe I actually do love God. Certainly some Christians do. Perhaps I do understand and willingly embrace what He is up to in my life. How, then, do I discern and appreciate the good that God is doing in me when bad things happen? How do I gratefully recognize the good He is working in my soul when life punches me in the gut? It won't do to distract myself from the pain, paste a saccharine smile on my face, and cheerily say, "God is good."

But Jesus seems to give us warrant to expect only good things from God. He once asked a crowd of would-be followers, "Which one of you, if his son asks him for bread, will give him a stone? Or if he asks for a fish, will give him a serpent? If you then, who are evil, know how to give good gifts to your children, how much more will your Father who is in heaven give good things to those who ask him?" (Matt. 7:9–11 ESV). What does God believe are good things? What good things is He giving us when bad things happen? These questions need to be asked.

During a routine medical check-up, the doctor spotted a suspicious-looking mole on my friend's back. "It looks benign," the doctor said, "but I want to make sure." My friend left the exam praying for the good news his physician expected. Lab results confirmed the mole was malignant melanoma. My friend asked God for bread. He was given a stone. He asked for a fish. God gave him a serpent. That is how my friend saw it. Again, the question needs to be asked: How does melanoma work together for someone's good?

Perhaps the good will only be realized in heaven. Religious people who believe in a good God typically anchor their ultimate hope in the God-promised good news that eternal bliss in paradise awaits true believers. In the light of eternity, Paul could see that his present troubles were small and wouldn't really last very long (see 2 Cor. 4:17). He didn't sugarcoat bad things, trying to make them taste sweet.

It's true, of course, that eternal happiness is understood differently in different religions. It might be an unfair caricature, but Muslims are famously known for eagerly anticipating heaven's joy as a sexual orgy, Hugh Hefner's undiminished pleasures lasting forever. Jews look forward to David's kingdom being restored to its glorious peak in a world governed for Israel's sake by Jehovah. Christians are alone in the confident hope of one day joining the dance of the Trinity, learning a few clumsily executed steps now, as we're being formed to relate like Jesus, and then living forever in perfect rhythm with the relational nature of the three-Person community of God in a world made perfect by Jesus. Think of it: actually loving God in every moment as our greatest good, and loving others without any stain of self-centeredness. It's coming. It will be ours to enjoy in a world without weeds.

Whether Muslim, Jew, or Christian, we worship a deity whom we believe will be up to something unspeakably good—*then*! But what good is God up to *now*, when melanoma is diagnosed, a child dies, a spouse proves unfaithful, or a job is lost? What good news does God have to share with us now as we live not only in a world rife with problems but also as people whose lives abound with difficulties and whose souls sometimes teeter on the brink of despair?

Muslims expect Allah's blessings in this life as they strictly adhere to Muhammad's teachings. Jews hear good news from Jehovah in their privileged opportunity to live now as God's chosen people who, despite severe persecution, will survive until Messiah comes (not Jesus) and secures Israel's rightful place in the world.

Christians hear God's good news for now, in this life, in the words of Jesus: "I came that they may have life and have it abundantly" (John 10:10 ESV). This abundant life is to be fully enjoyed in heaven but is also able to be substantially enjoyed now.

But what is "abundant" now in the abundant life Jesus came to give us? An abundance of good things? A stone instead of bread? A serpent rather than a fish? Disease when we wanted health? None of that makes any sense. Jesus led us to expect bread and fish from God. When Jesus returns to this world and makes everything new, there will be an abundance of good things that match our understanding of good things: no more tears, no more death, no more sorrow, no more crying, no more pain. Those are good things, for then (see Rev. 21:4–6).

But somehow we've gotten the idea that the "no mores" begin now; not completely, of course, but perhaps in limited form as "less thans." Shouldn't Christians at least have fewer tears, untimely deaths, sorrows, reasons to cry, and pains than others?

Without biblical warrant, modern Christian culture has been infected with false optimism. We have disfigured the gospel for today's entitled Christians into the good news of God's provision of abundant reasons to live most days with a sunny smile and no flirting with despair, to sing worship music full of upbeat praise with little room for lament, and to always have cause to relate to others with an upbeat spirit, thinking we best represent the Man of Sorrows with a chipper attitude.

God's good news *does* provide reason to smile through tears, to praise in the midst of lament, and to relate with hope even though discouraged. But the reason does not lie in a promise from God that the good things He loves to give us mean that life most often will go our way. Why do we sometimes assume that ongoing difficulties, continuing failure, and heartbreaking tragedies are anomalies in the Christian life? Have we come up with a gospel that tells us bad things really shouldn't happen to good people who are promised good things (as we understand the meaning of good) from our good God?

The risen Lord of life instructed Ananias to inform the newly converted Saul that He would "show him how much he must suffer for my name's sake" (Acts 9:16). And true to His word, the biblical story goes on to record hard times for Paul. Apparently Jesus believes bread and fish can be experienced in hard times. In his letter to the Philippian Christians, written some time after his conversion, Paul told them, "For you have been given not only the privilege of trusting in Christ but also the privilege of suffering for him" (Phil. 1:29). Trusting Christ? For what? For good times? Apparently not!

Years later, from a Roman dungeon, awaiting head-severing execution, Paul wrote his last words before death to young Timothy: "Everyone who wants to live a godly life in Christ Jesus will suffer persecution" (2 Tim. 3:12). Persecution is included in the good news that Jesus came to give us an abundant life? Small wonder that many of us are tempted (like Saul, as we shall see) to distort God's good news into news we can easily recognize as good and to deny any teaching to the contrary.

The temptation to distort and deny grows stronger as we listen to Jesus. Shortly before He died and then disappeared into the bliss of heaven, Jesus said this to His disciples: "Here on earth you will have many trials and sorrows." The context surrounding that dismal prophecy includes the encouragement to His followers to "take heart, because I have overcome the world" (John 16:33). What did He mean? He went on to offer the hope of peace, but a peace Jesus would provide in the presence of trouble, not its absence.

Everything I've so far written in this chapter leaves me no choice but to skeptically ask a question with a tinge of both cynicism that weighs down my soul and flickering hope that barely wards off despair:

What, then, is the good news from our good God about an abundant life of good things to be enjoyed while we live in the midst of trials and sorrow?

Peace

58

Before Saul became Paul, the man we know today as the greatest champion of the gospel of Christ, he looked for an answer to that question. He found one—because he distorted God's news into news he could relish without repenting of pride, and because he denied the meaning of whatever he heard from God that challenged his thinking. Saul came up with a wrong answer, a *counterfeit gospel*, a perversion of the story God was telling, a perversion that honored what Saul wanted, not what God had in mind.

I want now to take a brief look at Saul's life to understand how he arrived at such a wrenched, out-of-shape misrepresentation of God's good news. What we see in Saul may help us realize we're in constant danger of reducing the gospel into a message we can more easily believe is good.

Keep this in mind: God does have a wonderful plan for our life in heaven—wonderful because, with unmitigated delight, we will *enjoy* everything He then has in store for us. And He has a wonderful plan for our life now, on earth—wonderful because, with deep gratitude, we can *value* everything He is doing in us and through us in the midst of severe trials and acute sorrow.

Saul's Counterfeit Gospel

Through distortion and denial of Scripture, Saul came up with a counterfeit gospel that called him to a way of life he could perversely enjoy in this world.

In the biblical story, we first meet Saul when Stephen was stoned for following Jesus. "Saul was one of the witnesses, and he agreed completely with the killing of Stephen" (Acts 8:1). A brief review of what we know of Saul's background will help us see why he thought killing Stephen would please God.

Saul was born in Tarsus, a prosperous, university-type city located in the fertile region known as Celicia. His family was apparently well-to-do, allowing Saul to lead a privileged life from his earliest years. Although a Roman citizen, in later years he described how proud he had felt to be a Jew: "Circumcised on the eighth day, of the people of Israel, of the tribe of Benjamin, a Hebrew of Hebrews; as to the law, a Pharisee; as to zeal, a persecutor of the church; as to righteousness under the law, blameless" (Phil. 3:5–6 ESV).

Each one of those self-references is significant. Taken together they tell us that Saul, a Roman citizen with all the entitlements provided by Rome to its citizens, was a thoroughly committed purebred Jew. His status as an elite Jew meant more to him than his position as a Roman citizen. Although he was born in Tarsus, Saul was raised and educated in Jerusalem, mentored into Judaism by Gamaliel, the leading Pharisee of his day, and as his student thoroughly trained in Jewish laws and customs. As a young man, Saul became very zealous about honoring God in everything he did. His way of honoring God included, likely even centered in, persecuting "followers of the Way, hounding some to death, arresting both men and women and throwing them in prison" (see Acts 22:3–4).

The good news that Saul believed came from God might be summarized as follows:

- The Jewish religion alone is true.
- Jews are God's chosen people. Gentiles are not.
- All persons who refuse to comply with Jewish law and instead become disciples of Jesus, a patently false messiah, must be held accountable for slandering God.
- The cause of God is served by either imprisoning or putting to death all heretics who defy the truth of God by their submission to the teachings of Jesus.

Saul later realized he had terribly perverted God's good news. But why? Why did such a sincere, bright, zealous man fervently embrace a gospel that was no gospel at all? Why was he so vulnerable to the devil's deception? At least three reasons stand out:

- Saul was brought up in a *culture* committed to Jewish elitism.
- From birth, Saul was wired with a fiercely zealous *temperament*.
- Like every person born except Jesus, Saul came into this world with a *fallen soul*, naturally disposed to personal pride and entitled self-centeredness.

Children naturally embrace cultural ideas that fit their temperament and, equipped with a deceitful heart, distort those ideas into a worldview that frees them to live in a manner that provides them with a sense of purpose and fulfillment. Though blessed with a brilliant mind, Saul, without consciously realizing what he was doing, distorted the meaning of the Scripture he was studying to match what he wanted to hear; apparently he denied, or perhaps simply ignored, passages that could not be easily distorted, whose teaching threatened to lead him away from a gospel he could gladly embrace. The lesson for us?

Distort what you read in the Bible to fit your preconceived ideas; deny whatever you find in the Bible that strikes you as bad news; just don't think about it. Given your cultural background, your prewired temperament, and your fallen inclination to mangle God's thoughts to better match yours, you can be on your way to coming up with a counterfeit gospel that supports the way you naturally want to live.

The insidious influence of worldly culture (especially when it permeates our church culture), inbred temperament (that directs us toward a way to live and relate that feels true to who we are), and our inherited fallenness (that disguises distorted truth as true truth and justifies dismissively denying biblical teaching that makes no sense) work together to make us feel "comfortably Christian" with a counterfeit gospel.

Distorting the true gospel into what might be called good-enough Christianity and denying any call to radical discipleship as unreasonably severe leads us to travel on a broad road that promises a pleasant life but delivers a wasted life. A good-enough Christian life presents itself in many forms. Here are three:

- Husbands and wives who aim no higher than getting along well, enjoying life together, and gratefully receiving God's blessing; couples who give little active serious thought to what it would mean to put the Christ-church relationship on display by how they relate to each other.
- Parents who are happily satisfied when their children live moral, responsible, respectful lives and are blessed with adequate self-esteem and abilities to succeed in life; parents who provide God's Spirit with little opportunity to work through them to form their children into mature disciples of Jesus.
- Men and women, professing Christians all, who depend for fulfillment and happiness on family, friends, careers, and hobbies; people who relate well and are helpful to many but have little prayerful passion to draw others, both unbelievers and believers, to Jesus by how they love and relate.

The counterfeit gospel, then, in Saul's mind:

Eradicate Christianity and, with satisfying zeal, defend and promote Judaism.

The counterfeit gospel, now, in many Christians' minds:

Shrink Christianity into a good-enough life of morality, good values, friendly relating, and church involvement designed to win from God the good life of good things that define the abundant life. The obvious error of the health-and-wealth gospel is cleverly

*delivered in Christian-sounding ways that encourage Christians
to believe that every bad thing will become good, in this life.*

When God's ways don't make sense, we can respond like Jonah and resist and run. Or, like Saul, we can maintain the appearance of a God-honoring life by distorting God's ways that don't make sense to us into a Christian-looking understanding of His ways that do make sense to us, and we can casually deny biblical input that exposes the falseness of the gospel we have embraced.

But we can also choose to tremble and trust like Habakkuk—trembling when God's ways threaten to ruin our comfortable lives but trusting that God is always up to something that is soul-stirringly good.

4

Tremble and Trust (The Response of a Discerning Soul)

The Story of Habakkuk

The smaller story of our lives, the story we can watch unfold around us and in us, has many chapters, some pleasant, some hard. But in every moment God's larger story, visible only to the eyes of faith, is unfolding. We tremble in our own smaller story or we trust that God is telling a larger story, one that eternity will prove is good.

Listen to Paul's too often misunderstood words: "No test or temptation that comes your way is beyond the course of what others have had to face." Is that supposed to make us feel good? Misery doesn't always love company. "All you need to remember is that God will never let you down." Is Paul telling us that my friend's cancer, and mine, will be cured? He continues, "He'll never let you be pushed beyond your limit; he'll always be there to help you come through it" (1 Cor. 10:13 MSG).

Good news, we say. It appears that God's Word guarantees that nothing bad will ever happen to us beyond what we think we can endure. Does it? In earlier years, I've sometimes shared this with God: "It's okay if this happens, but not that. You've authorized me to set limits on what You allow." It's comforting to believe that nothing really bad will come into my life if I pray, tithe, and walk with Jesus.

Our capacity to fit Scripture into our understanding of how a good God should treat us is endless. We're not always interested in sitting under Scripture, willing to hear whatever God is saying to us through the inspired writers. The word translated "test" or "temptation" in the Corinthian passage carries the idea of provocation, speaking into a circumstance that provokes us to wrestle with a moral choice. Difficulties lead us to a crossroad, a choice point: Will we place priority on revealing God's nature as we respond to a troubling dilemma, or will we indulge our spirit of entitlement by doing whatever promises to change things for the better, or at least helps us to feel better, with little concern to honor God?

I hear Paul telling me this: *sin is never necessary to pursue your deepest well-being. It can, however, be effective in quickly but artificially promoting your sense of well-being.* Paul was in jail, awaiting execution. He could have renounced Jesus, avoided martyrdom, and been released from prison to enjoy a pleasant evening with friends. But his soul would have shriveled. Instead, Paul quite literally lost his life to save it, to live congruently with his deepest desire to love Jesus. For Paul, that was life.

Do we even think like that? Do I? Or am I inclined to soften Paul's teaching to make it more pleasing to my not-so-deep thirst? Am I more interested in a comfortable life than a *Christian* life? Have I not heard the call to radical discipleship? Have I reduced it to an easier call to follow?

Our lives hit a bump in the road, and we pray, "Lord, transform my life. Renew my circumstances. At least renew my emotions so

I can feel good." Such a prayer represents another self-serving interpretation of Scripture. Paul wrote these words to the church in Rome: "Do not be conformed to this world, but be transformed by the renewal of your mind" (Rom. 12:2 ESV). He is talking about our soul transformation, not the transformation of our circumstances. Paul is *not* saying that the soul transformation God's Spirit is intent on producing depends on renewing our circumstances into a more comfortable experience or renewing our emotions into more pleasant feelings.

Have we become today's version of the rebellious Israelites, who told their spiritual leaders, "Tell us what makes us feel better. Don't bore us with obsolete religion" (Isa. 30:10–11 MSG)?

For Paul, this "obsolete religion" declared the promise of soul transformation, relational formation, and learning to delight God by loving like Jesus even in the most difficult circumstances and while experiencing the most painful emotions. The work God has in mind to do in us depends on renewing our minds, changing the way we think. God thinks one way about what it means to live an abundant life. We think another way. Until our thoughts line up with His, relational formation will remain elusive.

Difficulties and distress present a one-of-a-kind opportunity to think like God and, guided by right thinking, to then live the abundant life of loving like Jesus. We must keep in mind that Jesus believed He was giving us good news. The process of seizing this good news opportunity looks something like the following.

The Process

Difficulties develop. Distress tags along. God seems so present when life moves along smoothly. But when we really need Him, the heavens too often go silent. Like me, perhaps you wake up many mornings around 4:00 a.m. Your mind races, reviewing your difficulties and feeling your distresses. Prayer seems pointless. You've realized God has not promised to repair what's wrong or to relieve your ache. You're on your own, wondering if you have the strength and wisdom to effectively handle your problems.

A Bible verse comes to mind: "Consider it a sheer gift, friends, when tests and challenges come at you from all sides" (James 1:2 MSG). How are you supposed to do that? "Don't try to get out of anything prematurely. Let it do its work so you become mature" (v. 4 MSG). You want to be mature. You know that's a good thing. But right now you want your life to go better so you can feel better. Can't you become mature in good times?

It's then the truth you reluctantly acknowledge hits you hard. It clutches at your throat. You realize God is not committed to providing the help you most want. He may. He may not. No guarantees on that front. What now? What to do? Where to go?

More good news! At least God thinks so. The stage is now set for His Spirit to get on with forming your soul. His Spirit is about to open a door into your well-protected, pride-barricaded soul, a door through which only Jesus, on behalf of His Father, can enter. This is *good* news?

I'm on that operating table. The Spirit's scalpel has twin edges: exposure that convicts and grace that enlivens. In my experience, God's work of penetrating into the depths of my soul and making me aware of what's there requires not only divine skill but also divine patience. I squirm. I'm not at all sure I'm prepared to deal with what lies buried in my center. If we become aware of what is hidden within us, beneath a thick layer of terror-driven pride, we somehow sense that we will get in touch with both emptiness, a compelling *desire* that nothing in this world can satisfy, and insolence, a *demand* to experience now a consuming pleasure under our control, a kind of pleasure God will not provide. The desire that we know is lodged deep in our souls somehow draws us; we perceive it to be strangely beautiful. The demand we've never been able to fully smother feels unarguably ugly. A thirst for beauty we only dimly see? An ugly demand to which we still yield? Better to live out of touch with what is inside us. To see what is there would make us uncomfortable, uneasy, and aware of foreboding angst.

Will we follow the Spirit as He leads us into our interior world, where a beautiful desire that will remain unsatisfied till death is about to be exposed, and where an ugly demand that, if indulged, will destroy relationships lies ready to shame us? Our choice is clear: to stiff-arm God, quenching His Spirit, or to seek God, keeping in step with His Spirit. If we make the wrong choice, the door into our soul remains closed till another time. Make the right choice and the door cracks open.

Let me now get quite personal. Several hours ago, when I awoke shortly after 3:30 in the early morning, the door to my soul began to crack open. No alarm had been set to wake me. The Spirit had work to do. I immediately began to toss and turn in bed. My mind was racing, and my stomach was knotted with worry. The forming process of soul-entering was underway.

I felt frustrated. I knew God loved me, yet He was allowing an impending minor catastrophe to remain impending. For more than an hour, I agonized over one prayer: "God, I know You're good. The cross leaves no room for doubt. But as I wrestle with real difficulties in my life, I need to know: *What good are You?*"

It wasn't pretty, certainly not pious, but I was seeking God. I could do nothing but present myself to Him as I was, not as I wished I were. The Spirit seized His opportunity. The door opened. I became freshly aware that I wanted to know God more than I wanted any lesser good. I felt the thirst in my soul to rest in His goodness when so much bad was going on in my life. And, reflected in the mirror of His holiness, I saw my double-mindedness. I professed my love for God but chased after good things in this world as if my life depended on having them. For a moment, I was in touch with my *best thirst* and my *worst problem*.

69

It is then, when we passionately realize how much we long to know God and love like Jesus, and when we see how we're scrambling to enjoy lesser goods, that we learn what it means to tremble and trust. We tremble to realize that the thirst in our soul will lead us on a journey where only sips of the living water we long for are available when we feel desperate for gulps. And we tremble at how inclined we are to demand full satisfaction now and to indulge whatever pleasure seems to provide it.

But then our thirst intensifies. Only deep trembling puts us in touch with deep thirst. We trust that the journey is leading us to springs of living water that never go dry and to enough sips from little springs along the way to know God is as eager to satisfy us as we are eager to be satisfied—more, actually. He is good!

And we learn to trust that every untrusting effort on our part to feel a kind of satisfaction that God does not make available to us, every sinful effort to manage the well-being of our soul, is not condemned. Christ was condemned in our place. We are free—not free to sin (though we will) but free to indulge our deepest desire that we're in touch with: to represent God well by loving like Jesus.

When God's ways make no sense, we then no longer resist Him by running toward a lifestyle of drinking gulps of what turns out to be dry water. Nor do we stubbornly distort the gospel into an opportunity to "feel Christian" as we satisfy ourselves on the good things available in this life. We no longer deny what is biblically clear, that God is calling us to be committed to the well-being of others at any cost to ourselves, a call energized by the consuming thirst to know God and to make Him known by how we relate.

That's a brief snippet from my ongoing story of wanting to respond well when God's ways make no sense to me. Unlike mine, Habakkuk's story is a fully God-inspired account of a man who learned to tremble and trust when God's ways baffled him. It's a story worth knowing.

The Story of Habakkuk

Habakkuk was utterly unsettled by God—twice. Jonah responded to God's disturbing ways by taking off without saying a word to God. Habakkuk stayed in relationship with God and made his feelings known. Unlike Saul, Habakkuk knew that when he and God had differing opinions on how best to deal with a bad situation, he needed to be quiet and listen to God. His rejoinder to God when God's ways unsettled him led him on a journey I want to take, from fear to faith. The end of his recorded story reveals a man who quivered and trembled over how God did things but unbendingly trusted God's goodness whatever He was up to. A brief review of the times in which Habakkuk lived will provide a needed backdrop for understanding his dialogue with God.

It seems likely to many biblical scholars that Habakkuk served as God's prophet in the latter days of King Jehoiakim's reign over Judah. No king of God's people was more evil. He was the king who brazenly cut up Jeremiah's scroll with his knife and threw the pieces into a fire. On the scroll, Jeremiah had written what God had told him, that Babylon would destroy Judah. Jehoiakim had no interest in hearing bad news from God (see Jer. 36:21–23). Under his leadership, Judah had declined into the most offensive forms of immorality, injustice, and violence. And Habakkuk saw it all. It grieved his godly heart.

When he sat down to write his story, the first words that flowed from his heart through his pen were, "The oracle that Habakkuk the prophet saw" (Hab. 1:1 ESV). The Hebrew word he wrote that we translate as "oracle" carries the meaning of a foreboding utterance of doom, perhaps similar to what Jeremiah wrote on the scroll that Jehoiakim refused to read. How could God endure such evil in His people? It was a burden too heavy for Habakkuk to bear. How much more troubling it must have been to God. Surely He would do something, perhaps call Habakkuk, as He called Jonah, to preach judgment as a stimulus to repentance. That's the background. Here's the story.

Chapter 1:2–4

Time passed, and God did nothing. No doubt Habakkuk had prayed. But no response. The same problem faces Christians today. How many Christian parents have had no choice but to see a child's laziness, disrespectful attitude, or outright rebellion, and to pray earnestly for God to reach their child's hard heart through their love and discipline? And things get worse. One mother recently told me, "I'd like to write a book titled *Parenting: The Death of a Dream*." In that same spirit, Habakkuk felt frustrated. "O LORD, how long shall I cry for help, and you will not hear?" (v. 2 ESV).

God's inaction in the face of sin that severely offended Him made no sense to Habakkuk. His impatient confusion got the best of him. He essentially confronted God: "God, are You faithful to Your holy character or not? If Your plan is to choose a Jewish nation to represent Your nature to the world, shouldn't You be dealing with all the sin I see among Your people? And yet You're doing nothing. I don't get it" (vv. 2–4, paraphrased).

Chapter 1:5–11

In His own time and way (neither of which usually match our expectations), God responds to His followers when they express puzzled concern over how He is telling His story. God replied to Habakkuk's challenge, but His words only increased Habakkuk's confusion. God's response came in two parts:

1. Habakkuk, brace yourself for a shock. Something is about to take place that you will find difficult to understand, something impossible to reconcile with your understanding of what I should do (v. 5, paraphrased).

72

2. The evil you've seen among My people is not nearly as depraved as the evil I see in Babylon. Yet I intend to use the more evil nation to punish the less evil nation (vv. 6–11, paraphrased).

What Habakkuk did not know was that the plan he heard included a design to do a good work in him, a work that God's Spirit would use to do a similar good work in countless others until Christ's return. God was prying open the door into Habakkuk's soul through his utter bewilderment over His ways. Habakkuk would soon recognize his proud demand that things should be done as he thought best. When the layer of pride that covered his soul was shattered, Habakkuk would realize he must tremble over God's ways and trust God's goodness in what He was doing.

Chapters 1:12–17; 2:1

At this point in the way God was working in his soul, Habakkuk was overwhelmed by the incongruity between who he knew God to be and what he realized God was about to do. He could have mimicked Jonah and simply resigned his role as prophet to such a frustrating God. Or, like Saul, he could have misrepresented what he heard from God and rounded up the worst of Judah's citizens, jailed them, then washed his hands of any feelings of guilt, thinking he was doing God's work. He did neither. Instead, he took a deep breath and reminded himself of who he knew God was, then squarely faced the apparent inconsistency between God's character and God's ways.

He spoke to God, acknowledging who he knew God to be. Habakkuk knew this:

- God is faithful to His promises (v. 12). He had made an unbreakable covenant with Israel. He would honor it.
- The eyes of God are holy. He cannot see evil and do nothing about it (v. 13).

73

But then he questioned God. God was allowing the Babylonians to keep living less like bearers of the divine image and more like brute savages. Verses 13 through 17 record Habakkuk's description of the degenerate, corrupt culture of the nation God would allow to destroy His own people. Yes, His people were sinful, but not nearly as wicked as this heathen country. It made no sense.

As too many do, Habakkuk could have given up on God. He could have shut down his mind, wrestled no more with his questions, closed his soul to any further word from God, and gone about managing his life as best he could.

But a dramatic shift took place. Habakkuk closed his mouth, uttering no further challenge, and opened his ears, eager to hear more from the God whose previous communication had disrupted him to his core. "I will take my stand at my watch post and station myself on the tower, and look out to see what he will say to me, and what I will answer concerning my complaint" (2:1 ESV).

I hear no arrogance in Habakkuk's words. I do not hear him saying, "Well, I'll give God a hearing. He may have a point or two I haven't thought of. But I'll still let Him know I don't much like His plan of action. Maybe I'll get through to Him." I hear nothing of the kind. Habakkuk has shifted from complaining to waiting. What was he not seeing? He was open to further revelation. He went to some trouble to climb to the top of a tower and listen. He sat quietly, high above his country, no longer focusing on the condition of his countrymen but now in position to hear God's thoughts and ways—thoughts and ways he could not hear in the noise of culture. I perceive a lesson in that for me.

Chapter 2:2–20

Habakkuk's soul, opened by difficulty and distress to hear God's larger story told, was eager now to listen to whatever God would say. Eventually, God did reveal Himself to a thirsty soul opened to listen.

What Habakkuk heard not only changed his life but also sketched a philosophy of history and revealed the path to life with God. In these nineteen verses, God delivered five messages:

1. Everyone who reads what I will now have you plainly write will find the strength to move forward into life with hope. No one need be paralyzed in despair by what I say (v. 2).

2. It may seem to you that I talk a good game but do nothing. But no! My story is always unfolding. Wait! On My timetable, the plot will become visible (v. 3).

3. Foolish people, those who live in always-deepening wickedness, manage their lives in the light of what they can see and what they can understand with their darkened minds. Wise people, grateful to be in right relationship with Me, walk through life in the light of what I reveal, according to a plan that by faith they believe is sovereignly good. Their life in Me, with Me, and for Me begins and continues by faith (v. 4).

4. I use evil people to further My purposes when I choose to. I owe you no explanation. But be assured: I use everything, good and bad, including the devil himself, to advance the beauty of My story. I will, however, without fail hold evil persons and nations accountable for their ugly pride and heinous deeds. Listen: I will now declare five woes against Babylon to let you know that My eyes are too pure to see evil and do nothing (vv. 6–19).

5. I call you, Habakkuk, and all My genuine followers, to be still and know that I am God (see Ps. 46:10). Habakkuk, be silent. You have no part in writing or directing the plot of My story. I do, however, privilege you with the call, a weighty and splendid opportunity, to advance My narrative chiefly by remaining faithful to Me no matter what trouble comes into your life that confuses and overwhelms you (v. 20).

Chapter 3:1–15

When Habakkuk heard God speak into the depths of his soul, beauty rose up within him and was expressed in the words Habakkuk spoke as the book he wrote comes to a God-pleasing end.

He offered a prayer, setting it to music so that generations to come, including you and me, could join him in the same prayer. The unusual word mentioned in his preface to the prayer—"A prayer of Habakkuk the prophet, according to *Shigionoth*" (3:1 ESV, emphasis mine)—likely refers to a lyrical psalm. Habakkuk was no longer complaining. He was now singing a song of lament and joy.

The next verse tells us that Habakkuk began his prayer by reflecting on the way God had led His chosen people up to this point in history. It would be well for us, like the prophet, to look back on visible evidence of God's faithful but sometimes unexpected and unwelcomed ways of working out His purpose in us and through us. Knowing the God of holy love was merciful even in judgment, Habakkuk was longing to see God *do His thing* (v. 2).

Habakkuk's mind, formerly filled with puzzled frustration over God's ways that made no sense to him, was now suffused with humble passion stirred by an awareness of God's *glory* (vv. 3, 4), His irresistible *power* (vv. 5–12, 14–18), and God's love for His unlovable people as evidenced by His unrelenting desire for their *salvation* (v. 13).

Chapter 3:16–19

Without Habakkuk's words recorded in these four final verses, his story would have little power to draw me into the privilege of telling God's story when His ways confuse me. Eliminate these verses and I hear nothing more than an exhortation to be quiet and let God do whatever He chooses, since He will do so no matter what I say or feel. But the prophet's last words attract me to God, to the God who really is working through all things for both my present and my eternal good.

> I trembled inside when I heard this;
>   my lips quivered with fear.
> My legs gave way beneath me,
>   and I shook in terror.
> I will wait quietly for the coming day
>   when disaster will strike the people who invade us.
> Even though the fig trees have no blossoms,
>   and there are no grapes on the vines;
> even though the olive crop fails,
>   and the fields lie empty and barren;
> even though the flocks die in the fields,
>   and the cattle barns are empty,
> yet I will rejoice in the LORD!
>   I will be joyful in the God of my salvation!
> The Sovereign LORD is my strength!
>   He makes me as surefooted as a deer,
>   able to tread upon the heights. (3:16–19)

As clearly as any other passage in Scripture, these verses reveal the morally excellent and personally advantageous response to God when His ways make no sense. That response can be summarized in two words: *tremble* and *trust*.

Tremble

Don't pretend everything is to your liking when it's not. Face the hard truth that God may allow terrible suffering in the lives of people He loves for at least two reasons. One, to prod us into waiting eagerly with grateful anticipation for the trouble-free life we will forever enjoy in heaven, with Jesus. Two, to discover the Spirit's power to love like Jesus in any circumstance of life or condition of soul and to thus tell God's story of amazing grace.

And we must remember: we live in a fallen world. Neither evil, famine, disease, nor hardship should surprise us. But too often we are surprised that God does so little to make things better. Many prayers for healing and protection go unanswered. And we tremble. Confidence in the goodness of God and the story He is telling must be rooted in Christ's promise to make everything new (see Rev. 21:5). Until then, we trust He is doing good in us and through us.

I have entered what today's culture calls the senior years. I feel their effect. I don't like it. I don't feel prepared for whatever is yet to come before I die. I am sometimes (happily not always) consumed by visions of possible dementia, life in a nursing home, chronic pain, lost opportunities to enjoy fatherhood and grandfatherhood, and, mostly, living without my wife if she dies before me. None of those anticipated difficulties are present realities. I gratefully enjoy the blessings still available. But thoughts of what old age might bring remain alive in me. And I tremble. Apart from hell later and abandonment now, God has not promised to protect me from any of what I fear but rather to supply the grace needed to persevere and live in hope.

I tremble in light of what may be coming. I tremble more before a God who will preserve my faith but, at least in some ways, will not protect my life as I wish He would.

I walk in the footsteps of Habakkuk. "I hear, and my body trembles; my lips quiver at the sound" of what is difficult now and what difficulties may yet be coming; "rottenness enters into my bones" at four in the morning, when my soul swarms with dread, and "my legs tremble beneath me" as I don't feel the strength I need to move on (Hab. 3:16 ESV).

Trust

"Yet I will quietly wait for the day of trouble to come upon people who invade us" (v. 16 ESV). Habakkuk is confident Babylon will be destroyed. And I realize: *suffering* *will not have the last word in my life.*

"Though the fig tree should not blossom, nor fruit be on the vines, the produce of the olive fail and the fields yield no food, the flock be cut off from the fold and there be no herd in the stalls, yet I will rejoice in the LORD; I will take joy in the God of my salvation" (vv. 17, 18 ESV). Even if every blessing that provides me with legitimately enjoyed comfort and happiness is removed, with Habakkuk I can trust God. For what? For the restoration of lost blessings? No, not in this life, but rather for the coming day of blessings without limit, and for the faith-wrought confidence that a good story told by a good God is invisibly unfolding now, even in my worst moments.

"God, the LORD, is my strength; he makes my feet like the deer's; he makes me tread on my high places. To the choirmaster: with stringed instruments" (v. 19 ESV). Only in difficulty do I depend on and therefore discover a strength I can remain ignorant of when I am living well in comfort. The strength I discover as I tremble empowers me to be surefooted as I walk on my high places of His call to live and love like Jesus as I trust that God "gives power to the faint, and to him who has no might he increases strength. Even youths [let alone seniors] shall faint and be weary, and young men shall fall exhausted; but they who wait for the LORD shall renew their strength; they shall mount up with wings like eagles; they shall run and not be weary; they shall walk and not faint" (Isa. 40:29–31 ESV). "And having done all," Paul tells us, we can "stand firm" (Eph. 6:13 ESV).

Imagine what it would mean, in the midst of difficult times and disappointing circumstances, to *fly* supported by the wind of God's story, to *run* the race set before us without succumbing to weariness, to *walk* the narrow road and not faint into a discouraged heap, and, having done all, to *stand* firm in the confidence that there is nothing better to do with our lives than to tell God's story of inscrutable love.

Fly, run, walk, stand: for a season, to fly with excitement as we follow Jesus, then to run with endurance a long race, then to walk with patience as troubles mount, and, as we near the finish line, to stand in hope.

Settled, growing trust is required to follow Jesus through every season of life. The needed trust develops only in souls that tremble. We must trust to obey. But we must tremble to trust.

As I write these words, I hear God asking me,

> How can you say the LORD does not see your troubles? . . .
> Have you never heard?
>   Have you never understood?
> The LORD is the everlasting God,
>   the Creator of all the earth.
> He never grows weak or weary.
>   No one can measure the depths of his understanding.
> (Isa. 40:27–28)

When God's ways make no sense, will we resist and run? Will we distort and deny? Or will we tremble and trust?

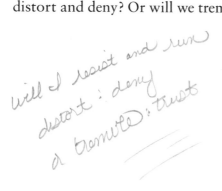

PART 2

When God's Ways Make No Sense, Tremble!

Why? What? How?

5

Why Must We Tremble
in Order to Trust?

I'd prefer a path to spiritual formation where trust eliminates trembling. Is ongoing trembling really necessary in order to achieve ongoing trust?

Reflect for a moment on the ease with which we glibly use the word *trust*. In the mind of the hearer, I suspect it usually arouses little more than wishful thinking. A few might be encouraged to momentarily feel a naïve optimism, to embrace another's well-intentioned but badly misguided confidence in God's goodness. "I'm trusting you'll have a safe flight," we say to a friend about to fly overseas. To an unemployed friend, we warmly offer, "I trust your job interview tomorrow morning will go really well."

When Christians speak of trusting that something good will happen, whether specified or not, the implication is clear: we're trusting God to bring about the good we desire. But neither of the two expressions of concern I listed, though no doubt sincere, provide more than unfounded hope. Neither points the other to the sure hope that God keeps His promises. For one simple reason: God promises neither a safe trip nor a new job.

In an important sense, prayer is different than trust. As my wife and I drive together to consult with my oncologist about the results from my latest tests, suppose I turn to her, rest my hand reassuringly on her arm, and say, "I'm trusting God for good news today." A very different sentence would be, "I'm praying we'll hear good news today." The difference in the two sentences matters.

Too often our version of trusting God carries with it an expectation of what God *should* do. We are, of course, to trust God to do all that He tells us in the Bible He will do. But this is where we sometimes get off-track. Without noticing it, we tend to trust God to do what we think a loving God ought to do. An honest look at what we mean when we use the word *trust* would likely turn up a subtle demand, a stubborn sense of entitlement to whatever good things we'd like God to give us.

Prayer for blessings, the if-it-be-Thy-will variety of prayer, must be grounded in surrendered trust, an undemanding conviction that God is advancing the good plot of His love story no matter what news the doctor brings, a plot that has our deepest well-being in view. Consider: fervent prayer for desired blessings must be offered on the altar of confident trust that God does all things well, even if the worst we fear happens.

The pairing of fervent prayer and confident trust has a way of creating an unsettling tension in us that exposes our spirit of entitlement and leads to repentance.

God, I so badly desire the good I'm now requesting. But I trust You to do what is best, for Your glory and my deepest well-being. And yet it feels to me as if my life depends on You giving me what I'm asking for. And I sense within me a real tension as I come to You with that request, knowing that in Your sometimes incomprehensible goodness and love, You may deny my

*request. May Your Spirit give me wisdom to know You will
never compromise Your commitment to lead me on the narrow road to life.*

We're freed then to distinguish between what we understandably
want God to do, for a sense of our immediate well-being, and what
we desperately *need* Him to do, for us to live the life that we most
want to live and to become the person we most long to be. And
that realization brings about the settled joy of knowing that God
has done, is now doing, and forever will do everything we need to
enjoy all that we were created to experience. Our love for the God we
come to trust then weakens our proud and foolish expectation that
He should cooperate with the script we've written for our smaller
story, a script that calls for blessings from God without a trust-based
relationship with Him on His terms.

As I write those words, I'm anticipating that you might be asking
the question that comes to my mind. Am I quibbling over words?
Prayer? Trust? Are they really that different? Perhaps I'm fussily asking for a kind of semantic precision that would plague us with an
obsessing conscience always whispering, *No, here you must use the
word* prayer, *not* trust. *But yes, there you can use* trust.

Yet even as I wonder if I'm making much over little, it becomes
clear to me that sloppy semantics can badly distort our understanding of what it truly means to say that God is good. We just received
word an hour ago that an already-agreed-upon and signed contract
to buy our house is now at some risk. Am I to *trust* God to see to it
that the sale goes through? Or am I to *pray* that it will? There is a
difference. Trusting God for an on-schedule closing that didn't happen would likely raise a hard-to-quiet question in my mind about
His loving goodness. Praying for a sale that didn't go through would
incline me to wonder exactly what good God was up to.

85

This point is important enough to justify three more illustrations.

An email pops up on your computer from a close friend. She just returned home from a routine medical check-up. The doctor felt a small hard lump in her breast. He suspects it's benign, but she must wait for the results of her needle biopsy. You write back, "I'm so sorry you have to go through this. Of course, you're nervous; I would be too. But I'm really trusting God that things will be okay." Two days later she replies: "It's benign! I'm so relieved. You were right. God is *so* worthy of trust." Six months pass. You've enjoyed many moments of happy fellowship with your friend, several during praise gatherings in church. Then late one afternoon another email arrives. "The doctor found a second lump. It's malignant and fast-growing. I'm really scared, and *so* disappointed." Now, together with your friend, what can you trust God for? Is He no longer worthy of your confidence in His goodness? What does His goodness guarantee?

Your younger brother's nineteen-year-old son has just been arrested for dealing drugs to support his habit. He's scheduled for a court appearance and will be tried as an adult. You meet your brother for coffee. "This has got to be tough. I can't imagine what you must be feeling. Somehow God's got to be in this. Listen, how about if right now we commit to trust God that your boy will really soon find the Lord, that this mess will wake him up and get him on a good path. And let's also trust God to provide a compassionate judge at his hearing." Your brother's weak smile and downward glance lets you know what he's thinking but won't say. *I appreciate your concern. But right now I don't know how to feel confident that my boy will turn around. We might as well trust God that I'll win the lottery.* In your mind, your brother's faith is stumbling. Discouragement has made him cynical. Do you now more passionately reassure him that he can trust God for the blessings he so badly wants?

And are you certain God will provide those blessings? If so, on what basis?

It's late February in Minnesota. It's already been a long winter. And another storm has just dumped a foot of snow on your driveway. The hired plow is right now straining to clear the way for tomorrow's drive to the airport. Your scheduled ten-day vacation in sunny Mexico beckons. The phone rings. Your best friend, who lives in Florida, is calling. "Just checked the internet for weather in Cabo: 84, blue skies, no clouds for a week. Remember what I told you? I'm trusting the good Lord to push back any storms the devil might be sending. You deserve a break from all the bad weather you've been having. God knows you need it." Eight days later, huddled with your wife in what you thought would be a larger, nicer room at the resort for which you paid top dollar, you look up from your novel to see heavy rain pouring down for the sixth straight day. Your friend's words come to mind. You're serious about your Christian faith. But right now you're wondering—is the good Lord good or not? You remind yourself about Christ's death. You *know* God is good. But you're asking, *I know He's good, but in this moment what is He good for?* You're not sure. You pour yourself a third cup of coffee and lower your eyes back to the novel. At least John Grisham tells a good story.

If we're going to trust God to keep His promises, we'd better be clear about what promises He's made. But if we're trusting that God is somehow obligated by love to grant, if not every request we make, then at least the most desired ones, the ones that really matter, then we've set ourselves up to be disappointed by God, to question His goodness. And the effect of trusting God for good things He has not promised to provide can impact how we pray. Our prayers can become a kind of negotiation: "God, I'll do this if You'll do that." Or, a bit more piously, "You've done that because

I did this." We have several strategies for managing God. None work too well.

We will not understand what it means to tremble in a fashion that births trust until we come to grips with the disturbing truth that the larger story God is telling does not always follow the script we've come up with for our smaller story. The all-powerful, sovereign God who loves us as no one else can is the same loving God who so often frustrates our expectations. On His watch we may develop Alzheimer's or contract cancer or endure an unwanted divorce. Christians beheaded in the Middle East are no less loved than those of us who live in safer surroundings. Can we sing "Great Is Thy Faithfulness" no matter what happens? How? What will we mean as we sing the words of that hymn?

If we're to follow Jesus on the narrow road to what He thinks of as life, we must discover a kind of trust that

sustains us in worship during our darkest night,

frees us to love others when others fail us, and

anchors us in seemingly irrational hope and inexplicable joy, even when our souls are drowning in anguish.

The path to settled trust is marked by unsettled trembling. But why? Why must we tremble in order to trust? The answer requires careful thought.

6

Trembling

The Gateway to Trust

God is always doing us good. But what is the good He is doing?
Only an awareness of our deepest thirst frees us to correctly
answer that question.

Counterfeit Christianity has its appeal and is strong enough to draw unsuspecting Christians away from truth. In various forms, it has led many into error since the earliest days of the church. One form, however, seems especially popular today, attracting many not by its apparent correctness but rather by its compelling winsomeness.

In religious circles, what becomes counterfeit typically begins with unquestioned truth. Often deceiving themselves, false teachers subtly corrupt the implications of the truth they affirm and come up with a well-received but dangerously misleading message.

Clever counterfeiters in Bible-teaching churches ground their message in what the Bible emphatically declares—that God is love. The aged apostle John said so in his first letter to the church, written about sixty years after Christ returned to heaven. John had listened to Jesus teach. He had seen Jesus relate with people. As a close friend, John had spent time with Jesus. He saw the love of the Father displayed in the love of the Son. He watched Jesus die. He knew firsthand that God is love (see 1 John 4:16). When false teachers today declare that God is love, they speak the truth. Love was fully displayed when Christ died to give us life. Never has perfect love done such peerless good.

Then, with biblical warrant, they go on to teach that God never stops revealing His love by doing us good. Through His prophet, God told His people, "For I know the plans I have for you . . . plans for good and not for disaster." And again, "I will never stop doing good for them," referring to people He loves (Jer. 29:11; 32:40).

We listen and quite properly nod our heads in grateful agreement, ready to hear more. The teaching continues. We can therefore confidently trust God to do us good when life threatens to do us bad. No need to fear what evil can bring into our lives. Even when a door is opening to tough times, under God's control another door is swinging open to the good times He loves to provide. More than head nodding is now called for. We raise our hands. We love the teaching. It rings true. Better, it feels good.

We're approaching a slippery slope, but the slope looks level, firm, and stable. The foundation of truth has been laid. Rich soil has been plowed for the seeds of love to sprout. God is love. He is always doing us good. When life turns bad, good is on the way.

Now the lie is heard, perhaps not spoken directly but clearly assumed. It is this:

The good that God promises to do for us is the good we long for most.

Catch the implication. We can trust God to do what we mere humans think a good, loving, all-powerful God would do. A winsome, appealing, and comforting thought—but not true. Remember, Habakkuk thought God should straighten out Israel, not destroy them at the hands of Babylon. God thinks like us? The Bible says otherwise. "'My thoughts are nothing like your thoughts,' says the LORD" (Isa. 55:8). There are times I so strongly want to believe my thoughts line up nicely with God's. As I write these words, my wife will soon schedule recommended surgery; not a major procedure, says the doctor, but he reminds us that all surgery has its risks. Can I trust God to do us good?

In my mind and heart, "good" means successful surgery, brief and comfortable recovery, and long-term health with no need for follow-up treatment. It's difficult to imagine a lesser outcome that could be better or one that could do better good for my wife and me. Counterfeit Christianity has its appeal. It assures me that the good I want is the good God will do. I can therefore trust God for the outcome I pray for.

Genuine Christianity tells me something different. I can *pray* for the good I want. God will hear me, and He might answer my prayer. I'll thank Him if He does. I'll tremble if He doesn't. But I'm to *trust* Him for good as He understands it. Could there be a better good accomplished through an outcome to surgery that I prayed against? If so, a dramatic shift in how I think is required. Am I to believe that whatever advances the plot of the story God is telling has my deepest well-being in view? Genuine Christianity insists the shift must be made from self-comforting naïve trust to God-honoring wise trust.

Naïve Trust

Counterfeit Christianity approves a kind of trust that denies to God His sovereign authority to love me as He deems best. Naïve trust assumes that divine power will be exercised in a way that reflects my understanding of what a loving God would do. Christians so deceived trust God to provide the blessings that their own wisdom determines are essential to their deepest well-being and joy. Naïve trust rests in the hope that God is committed to honoring the script we've written for the smaller story of our lives, the story that begins at birth and ends in death.

Obviously, faith is needed if we're to trust that an outcome we cannot control will go our way. But the faith needed to bolster naïve trust is never supplied by the Holy Spirit. Such faith is untroubled and calmly optimistic, no trembling required. It is a credulous faith that assumes God agrees with our idea of what is good and on those terms will do us good. That kind of faith is supplied by our unholy flesh, a source of thinking that delights in foolishness, believing lies are true.

But God is telling a larger and bigger story that is wiser and better and longer lasting than the smaller story we script in line with our limited, time-bound perspective. The love story He has authored is guided by divine thinking that in so many critical ways is nothing like our human thinking. Is it not possible that an infinitely wise, graciously loving, and supremely powerful God could somehow be working a greater good than we can imagine through all the disappointments and difficulties that come our way? Can we now confidently hope that the good He is doing is advancing through every moment, and that it will be put on brilliant display later, to be fully enjoyed forever?

Counterfeit Christianity steers us away from such questions. Asking them can be too depressing, too unsettling, too difficult to answer with joy. Genuine Christianity invites us to wrestle with these questions. Perhaps there really is a surpassing good that our souls are most thirsty to enjoy, a good that we struggle to believe is good but that God is relentlessly committed to provide. And perhaps God can only orchestrate the good we most long for when lesser goods are sometimes withheld, when painful badness sometimes darkens our sky.

It is then we tremble; we cry out in confusion and agony, "God, what are You doing? We know You're good. You died to give us life.

But what You're now allowing doesn't feel like life. God, You're good, but right now in this terrible moment, *what are You good for?*" Trembling in the presence of a God who makes no sense presents the opportunity for God's Spirit to quiet our souls in wise trust.

Wise Trust

Trust that leads us toward joy is rooted in truth that no one naturally believes, the truth that our supreme good is the enjoyment of God as He is, not as we might wish Him to be. Even when God seems distant, unresponsive, and indifferent to our pain, wise trust is confident that He is doing us good, the good of doing what must be done to draw self-centered, proud people closer to Himself.

Faith that kindles wise trust is not untroubled; it is trembling faith that confesses that our good God will not cooperate with our thoughts of what is good. Though wobbly at times, the faith that supports wise trust knows that our understanding of goodness must line up with God's if we're to enjoy His confusing ways. But that shift will not develop easily. Can good emerge while injustice continues? Is God doing us good when a cancer grows that He could remove?

As a young Christian psychologist, I used to believe that following God's principles guaranteed the good we desire. During a break in a seminar I was leading, a couple in their fifties requested time to discuss heartbreak over their young adult son. I sat down with them, brimming with confidence that I could direct them to biblical principles of parenting that would restore their son to be a source of joy. "How can I help?" I asked, certain that I could. "Last week our son committed suicide," I was told. "We cannot bear the guilt, the shame, the loss." My mouth was stopped. I had never imagined that God's good plan could continue in the worst of times.

I now believe that wise trust in God's goodness quietly develops when His ways make the least sense. Only when false trust dies will true trust live. When we tremble over the ways of God that seem to bring nothing good into our lives, our descent into darkness creates the opportunity to land on brightness, on the truth that through all things God is working to accomplish the good that heaven will reveal we have always wanted to enjoy.

Why is that truth so difficult to believe? Why the fierce struggle to trust that God is always doing us good? The answer seems clear:

We are not in touch with the deepest thirst in our souls for the greatest good that God provides.

We ask too little because we want much less. We live, not to know God but to use Him to arrange for what we believe is the good we most want: good family, just treatment from others, emotional health. The list is long.

The tragedy is real. *Our desire for things to go well in the smaller story that begins at our birth and ends at our death is stronger than our longing to know God well enough to live now in His larger story, a story that began for us when we were born again and will continue throughout eternity.* A foolish tragedy: we thirst more for lesser goods than for the greatest good.

Our foolishness must give way to wisdom. It is right to enjoy the blessings of life that God provides, whether good weather on a day scheduled for golf or restored health after surgery. But if we're to live in wise trust, the shift must be made. Our thirst to know God must become stronger than our thirst for anything less.

But how does that happen? What is our part in the process? And what is God's part? Those questions bring us to the point of this chapter: only when we tremble before a God whose good ways do not seem good to us can we get in touch with our deepest thirst, with the inconsolable longing to know and experience God in a way we never will till we lay eyes on Christ.

We must passionately and continuously ask hard questions that confront us with a choice we must make. When we tremble in agonizing confusion over what our good God is good for, we must decide:

- *Will we resist and run*, like Jonah, searching for a better life than God provides?
- *Will we distort and deny*, like Saul before he became Paul, embracing a congenial version of counterfeit Christianity?
- *Or will we tremble*, refusing to turn away from the God whose thoughts and ways are higher than ours and instead wait patiently *in wise trust* for the Spirit to arouse the deepest thirst in our souls, the thirst to know Jesus, and through Him to know the Father's love and the Spirit's power, the thirst that genuine Christianity promises to quench in measure now and fully forever?

As we tremble in the presence of a God who makes no sense to our small minds, the questions we ask do something good in us. Cracks develop in the proud crust over our souls that we had no idea was there, a crust that both suffocates our longing to know God and permits us to feel only those desires for less than God Himself. Those cracks create space for the previously quenched Spirit to move into our inmost being and to excite the thirst for God that He earlier placed within us when we accepted the gift of life with Him.

Trembling when God's ways make no sense (and every honest Christian will encounter those ways) begins the shift from naïve trust to wise trust. It is a long and difficult shift away from the attractive lies of counterfeit Christianity that promise happiness in our flesh and deliver misery to our spirit, a shift toward the truth of genuine Christianity that arouses the thirst we can depend on God to quench with sips of living water now and full gulps later.

Trembling in the presence of a God who seems to disappoint us is the gateway that opens our souls to embrace God-honoring and God-dependent trust in His goodness. We trust even when His loving ways provoke confusion, fear, and anger in our still-maturing minds. Trembling leads us to discover the thirst we can trust God to satisfy. There is no stronger thirst.

7

A Hands-Off God?

God is never more near to us than when He seems most distant from us.

I woke up this morning once again feeling empty, listless, dutifully willing to do what needed doing—and mildly irritable. I wanted to feel full, full of hope that today would go well with no hassles, full of faith that God would smooth the way and provide whatever good was necessary to make today a good day, and full of love that would enable me to move toward people in a fashion that would allow me to feel good about myself as a follower of Jesus. Isn't that the Christian life God calls us to live? Isn't that the life the gospel makes possible?

I wanted to feel full. Instead I felt empty. As I climbed out of bed I felt most eager to fill my stomach with bacon and eggs and hot coffee.

I don't like feeling empty. To feel out of touch with whatever good God is doing in me and wants to do through my life reminds me that I have yet to travel some distance on the road to becoming who the Spirit longs for me to be.

But I'm on the road. I welcome the void in my soul, not because it's good in itself but because it creates an opportunity for me to get in touch with what's alive in the deepest region of my Spirit-indwelt soul.

The Emptiness

Felt emptiness is a telltale symptom of unquenched thirst, of strong desires that yearn for satisfaction that doesn't come, satisfaction God could provide in fullness but offers only in tastes. Embracing that emptiness and letting it guide me into the territory within me where I thirst for God above all other goods keeps me on the narrow road when God, as He does so often, denies me lesser goods I greatly want.

I could run from the emptiness. By responsibly getting on with my busy day, I could pay no attention to my cry for fullness. I could choose to shush the cry and do something that would deliver a moment of felt satisfaction instead. In either case, I would remain out of touch with my soul's pure thirst for living water, my longing to know God, and remain in touch with a lesser, impure craving for a satisfying fullness I could manage on my own.

Because I am a Christian, buried deep inside me is a desire to know God that is stronger than my appetite for anything less. It's a matter of the highest importance that I become acutely aware of that hidden longing, for this reason:

A thirst for God, keenly felt, will sustain me more in my pursuit of God than either blessings from God or the experience of God.

Is that really true? Of course, nothing could more strongly sustain us than a deeply satisfying experience of God's presence and love. But that experience will never be fully felt until we see Jesus; the incomparable joy of experiencing God is not reliably available now to our still-forming souls. But a thirst for God, a thirst to know

98

Him in all His love and beauty, lies in the soul of every Christian and can be felt by every self-aware Christian. Our thirst stirs us to live in the sure hope of the coming day when we will thirst no more. Until then, our thirst to enjoy life in the next world sustains us with hope as we continue to live in this fallen world.

Wanting to feel my thirst for God, however, has its dangers. My inbred self-centered nature dies a slow death. Still alive, it can manage to lead me off-track. I might interpret my God-thirst to be a legitimate expectation that I will receive from God what I determine would be best for me rather than recognizing my thirst as a Spirit-shaped desire for whatever my loving Father sovereignly chooses to provide.

We all long for much more than God promises to provide in this life. When those longings go beyond the obvious good things of life—a loved one's restored health, freedom from depression, a decent job—and we feel an intense wish to more quickly advance in our spiritual formation or to more often delight in God's felt presence, it can then be difficult to accept that God may not answer those worthy prayers.

As an old children's chorus I used to sing assures me, "God can do anything but fail."[1] He could speed up the process of maturity. He could grant a palpable sense of His loving presence at all times. And yet too rarely do I clearly see His hand in the details of my life. Too little do I feel His strong hand in mine. At some point in a Christian's spiritual journey, it will become evident *God is a hands-off God*—not always, but often enough to leave His followers trembling.

I've become aware of something going on in me that is painful to own and even more painful to confess. It encourages me to know that saints far more saintly than I, including C. S. Lewis, have made similar confessions. My version is this:

I have no fear of coming to a point where I deny God's existence, but I do fear I might not be drawn to the God I discover Him to be.

When I most long for His tender involvement in my life, there are times when He seems to disappear and leave me with no choice but to realize He can be a hands-off God. It is then I experience a despicable urge to back away from Him, an urge that feels defiantly warranted.

Paul did better. Like me, he thirsted for what only heaven would provide. He told us that "if in Christ we have hope in this life only, we are of all people most to be pitied" (1 Cor. 15:19 ESV). God did not deliver him from enduring beatings, shipwrecks, snakebites, moments of impatience, or loneliness. Whatever trembling Paul experienced somehow moved him toward an unshakable confidence in God's goodness.

Fullness for Paul did not mean either a full supply of blessings that made his life comfortable and his ministry untroubled or a full experience of God's presence. For Paul, fullness meant to be filled with the knowledge of God's will and to be fully pleasing to God (see Col. 1:9–10). Paul knew that kind of fullness even as the emptiness in his soul longed to know Christ more deeply (see Phil. 3:10). For Paul, emptiness developed into hope as he waited eagerly for the day when his groaning soul would know only joy (see Rom. 8:23). Until then he trusted God to every day renew his commitment to remain faithful to the Lord's call on his life.

Christ is in us, arousing our hope for unspeakable glory when He makes everything new. "The experience of Christ dwelling in our hearts by faith gives us not the possession but the promise of full salvation. *The greatest gift of Christ in the present is hope for the future.*"[2]

Until that eternal day dawns, God will be revealed to our senses as a hands-off God in ways that will make no sense to us and at times will frustrate and even anger us. We will wonder why our loving Father does not open His hands wide to pour into our souls and lives all the blessings that by *His design* we long to experience. It is then, as we feel the emptiness in our souls, that the God of the Bible appears to bear some resemblance to the God of the deists.

100

Revised Deism?

Recently, I've been worrying close friends—and worrying myself—by admitting that I'm coming to see myself as a Christian deist. Christian deism? Isn't that an oxymoron? Wouldn't a Christian deist be attempting to bring together two contradictory systems of thought, two ways of viewing God's role in our lives that cannot mesh? It would seem so.

Christianity declares the good news that God never abandons us. He remains actively involved in our lives, always doing us good. Deism teaches that God made the world, created us to live in it, and then took off back to heaven, leaving us to fend for ourselves as best we can.

I am a Christian. Tested in my convictions for more than fifty years of thinking and rethinking the truth of all I claim to believe, I can now neither escape nor deny my firm conviction that God is good. The cross settles the question.

But life as I experience it makes me wonder: Could it be that God, now living in restored divine community since the resurrected Christ returned to heaven, is *not* doing all the good for Christ's followers that His death made possible? It sometimes looks that way, on two levels: what happens *to* people and what happens *in* people.

Just this morning I received a letter from a woman in her early fifties. Millie (not her real name) has been a committed Christian since coming to Christ in her teenage years. She never anticipated what God would allow.

A decade ago, her loving brother died a slow, painful death despite Millie's fervent prayers for his quick entrance into heaven.

One year ago, her apparently healthy son was admitted to the hospital with severe abdominal pain. He died the next morning. The autopsy revealed stomach cancer that, if identified earlier, could have been successfully treated. But no symptoms triggered a thorough medical exam.

Shortly after her son's death, Millie's distraught daughter, for twenty years a visibly sincere follower of Jesus, angrily declared she could no longer believe in a good God. It was time, she felt, to come out with a long-held secret. She announced she was a lesbian.

A month before Millie wrote me, her father, a healthy Christian man in his eighties, took his own life.

On one level, where bad things happen *to* Christian people walking with the Lord, what good can we trust that God is doing? What good is God up to in Millie's life? We often glibly retreat behind the statement "God is in control." Of what? Eliminate heaven and nothing makes sense. All is random, without meaning.

There is another level to consider, where troubles *in* us remain unresolved.

Rick feels impatient. He is now recognizing how committed he is to managing his life. "Trouble comes, and I fix it. I feel shame over my irritation with someone, and I hide behind a pleasant smile. I come across to everyone as a nice guy, but I'm seeing that I'm afraid to invest deeply in anyone's life. If I tried, it would become visible that there's not much to me."

Months of Christian counseling followed by months of spiritual direction have accomplished little. "I'm doing my part. Why isn't God doing His?"

Paula was adored as a little girl. Her devoted father was reliably with her, encouraging her, believing in her, always letting her know how special she was. Now an adult, Paula sees how she dismisses others, mostly her husband, as beneath her and worthy of little respect. "I feel such pressure to be seen by everyone as special, competent, likeable, and wise. I hate how defensive I get when someone sees my weaknesses. I've been a Christian now for more than thirty years. Whatever's wrong inside me is still wrong. Why isn't God doing more work in me?" Prayers for God's transforming work have gone unanswered.

102

Has God backed off from Rick and Paula? Couldn't He be doing whatever good in each of their lives is needed for them to enjoy evidence of their maturing? Christianity insists that when God seems to back off from doing good in someone's life, He is behind the scenes doing a greater good that will one day become visible. Deism believes we must resign ourselves to the fact that God has indeed backed off, indifferent to our concerns, with no intent to involve Himself in our lives. The divine watchmaker made the watch, set the gears in motion, then left it to run on its own. Some watches manage to keep good time. Others don't. That's the way it is.

Does Christianity allow for the thought that our good, loving, sovereign God, who is in control of all that happens, freely chooses to let nature, the nature of a weed-filled world and the nature of self-centered fallen people, run its course? And might that seem to us as if God has backed off from involvement in our lives?

The God of the Bible is no distant deity. He is a near-to-us God, a three-Person-one-God who is always doing good for His children. There is no need to revise our core Christian beliefs to accommodate our experience that sometimes screams, "Where is God? He's doing nothing. He is a hands-off God!"

Mere Christianity, C. S. Lewis's term for beliefs that must be held if we're to justify our claim to be Christian, in summary form is rooted in a three-part confidence:

1. God the Father created us with a plan for us to be happy living in a very good world.

2. God the Son put the plan into obvious motion when He became a sinless human and died for sinful humans, a choice made necessary by our insane decision to come up with our own plan for our happiness that we could implement.

3. God the Spirit now lives in Christians to convince us the Father's plan is good and on-track, even when bad things happen to

us and difficult things continue in us. And He nourishes faith to believe the Father's plan will culminate in a good, eternal climax beyond our ability to imagine.[3]

I am an unrevised Christian. I still struggle to believe, but doubt no longer has a grip on my mind. And I am a revised deist, someone who believes God does back away from us but who also believes He never backs away from us in indifference or with unloving intent. The essence of my belief as a revised deist is this:

God does back off from doing much of the good we think a good God should do, making the choice that is within His control to accomplish a greater good by denying us a lesser good.

We being the key word.

In a fallen world, we have every reason to expect trouble of some sort every day, whether a crashed computer, a toothache, or a much more severe calamity. And, of course, it is true that our sovereign God could make all things in this world as they should be, right now. But that day is not yet. In His sovereign will, He allows bad things to happen—until then. And we're to trust that nothing will happen now that God cannot work together for the good He longs for us to enjoy.

But isn't that conviction within the scope of Christian truth, consistent with the thoughts and ways of God? Of course. So why must I confuse things by referring to that belief as revised deism? For one reason: *Christians have a hard time believing in a Christianity that allows for God to sometimes come across as a hands-off God.* We prefer to believe that the loving God who is in control of everything will always do us the good we need in order to never question His goodness. We would rather not tremble. Naïve trust, the product of faith that assumes our thirst for the blessings we need to be comfortable will be quenched in this life, requires no trembling in God's presence, only naïve confidence in His goodness.

But the good we desire is not always the greatest good God is doing. On our journey through life, there will be times when we will tremble before a hands-off God.

~~~

A question presses itself into my mind as I reflect on what I have written here:

What does it mean to believe God is in control?

We naturally assume that a God who is in control, if He is good, will do for us the good we desire.

How, with any coherent consistency, can I claim to believe in the Christian God who promised to never leave nor forsake us and, at the same time, believe in some version of the hands-off God of the deists? In chapter 10, I will trace the journey that has brought me to this conviction: *the hands-off God is never more near to us than when He seems most distant from us.*

8

Hands-Off but Present
(And Still in Control)?

Only when life hauls us beyond an easy-to-maintain faith that
God is good will we discover a Spirit-granted faith that keeps
us steady during life's earthquakes.

Because God chose Paul to tell people the good news of Jesus, he
was now suffering in prison. Awaiting certain execution, Paul
wrote a letter to his young friend and disciple Timothy. In it he said
this: "I am sure that he is able to guard what I have entrusted to him
until the day of his return" (2 Tim. 1:12). What was Paul trusting
God to guard?

Facing death in the midst of intolerable circumstances, Paul continued to believe that a good God was in control of his life. He was
trusting God—to do what? A few thoughts:

- Why would telling people good news from God get Paul in
  trouble? Why would sharing good news get anyone in trouble?
  Is it possible that, for some reason in our makeup, we can hear

107

God's good news as bad news? Is that what happened in Paul's time? Could it happen today?

- Of course, we welcome the good news that we cannot earn a spot in heaven by living without sin. No one can. Jesus paid the price necessary for a holy God to grant us the undeserved gift of a relationship with Him that culminates in living with Him forever in paradise. Only the proud will deny the goodness of that news.

- But the news that a Christian's life in this world is guaranteed to include bad times, and that in these bad times joy is somehow made available, is difficult to hear as good news. Aren't the hoped-for blessings of life required for joy?

- One of the great temptations in churches today is to soft-pedal the Lord's promise that "Here on earth you will have many trials and sorrows. But take heart, because I have overcome the world" (John 16:33). Wouldn't we have wanted to be told that in His goodness and great power God would prevent, or at least keep to a minimum, the hardships of life?

- To appeal to their listeners, preachers have been known to revise the good news that Jesus actually announced to ensure that it comes across as good news to our entitled way of thinking. Our thoughts are not much like God's. Does our understanding of what constitutes good news square with God's?

True tickling the ears.

After years of hard times and suffering extreme physical discomfort and heartbreaking loneliness in a Roman dungeon, Paul felt sure that God would see to it that what he most valued was never taken away from him. And yet he had no confidence that his life would go well; he knew that God could not be counted on to provide him with the good things of life until he died.

What on earth had Paul entrusted to God with grateful and joyful certainty that He would faithfully guard until Christ's return?

As we commonly understand the term, life was not going well for Paul. And yet it was well with his soul. Why?

He answered that question in his letter to the Philippians.

> I have learned how to be content with whatever I have. I know how to live on almost nothing or with everything. I have learned the secret of living in every situation, whether it is with a full stomach or empty, with plenty or little. For I can do everything through Christ, who gives me strength. (Phil. 4:11–13)

Paul heard good news from God in the middle of bad times that God did nothing to improve.

A deist assumes that a God who does nothing to make the bad things better is uninvolved with us. A Christian deist admits that God can seem uninvolved when difficulties continue but believes God is always near, providing what we need to advance the story He is telling. As a Christian deist, I trust God's loving involvement in my life even as I tremble over difficulties He does nothing about.

What was the "everything" that Paul could do in Christ's strength, whether beaten or shipwrecked or languishing in solitary confinement while waiting for the executioner's sword? The answer to that question reveals Paul's secret of contentment and lets me know how I can live well in good times and bad. Do I want to know the answer? Will I receive it as good news when I hear it?

Paul learned to tremble and trust—to tremble in the worst of times with no promise of relief till heaven and trust that God was doing something in him and through him that he most valued, even as God was doing nothing to soften Paul's suffering in this life. Whatever good God was working in Paul's circumstances enabled him to do everything he longed most to do. What was the "something good" still going on in him in the worst of times that freed him to do everything that made his life worthwhile?

Paul was sure that God was able to guard what he most wanted God to guard until his death. In that confidence, Paul trembled and trusted.

A Hard but Good Place

Three somewhat distinct phases of my journey through life as a hopefully forming Christian, phases I will describe in chapter 10, have brought me to where I find myself today, in what I experience as a hard place but feel mostly confident is a good one. The long journey has been plagued with the blessing of many questions that have stirred much confusion. The question harassing me now seems more disquieting than my earlier ones.

And yet, looking back over seventy-plus years, I have no doubt that a gentle hand has been guiding me through all the questions on to a good destination. And it seems clear that the same good hand is leading me to explore the next question, one that till now I have not seriously asked, a question that if seriously answered promises to carry me further on the path to where I long to go, to a place of soul rest in a restless world where I have been living too long as an unrested soul. I am confident that this Spirit-directed journey is moving me toward sustained, deeper joy, the joy of more often loving God and others well with the assurance that in any circumstance of life and in any condition of soul God is doing in me and through me the good I most want Him to do.

The narrow road seems to be getting narrower. The new question I'm asking is provoking new confusion, a nervous confusion that threatens to upend my understanding of what it means to call God good, what it means to trust Him to do me good. What is it that I am to entrust to His loving and sovereign control?

Given my present confusion, I feel the need to remind myself (and my family, friends, and readers) that the core "good news" convictions of Christianity's gospel are not at risk. Certain truths, however assaulted even now, are settled in my mind. Beliefs that form the foundation of biblical Christianity, which I embraced as a child, have stayed intact. I am still convinced that the Bible is true, that Jesus loves me, and that I will wake up in heaven when I die. After sixty years of my journey, these foundations of faith remain unchanged and firm. At least till now.

With some apprehension, I find myself willingly but only sometimes eagerly following the Spirit's nudging to travel into an unfamiliar place. I am questioning something that for years I confidently but unthinkingly assumed to be true. Is God in control? *Of course*, I've uncritically replied. But a perplexing uncertainty has risen in my mind about the nature, extent, and felt experience of God's loving involvement in a Christian's life. This new hesitancy is steering me into unsettling regions of thought.

I've noticed that Christians whose lives are moving along nicely have little real interest in the question. As long as life's blessings continue with only manageable setbacks, the standard answer seems happily true: our wonderful God is controlling things to our satisfaction. Perhaps it is my advancing years with worrying health concerns that are the tools the Spirit is using to rouse the questions in my mind.

Unanswered Questions

Christian deism, a term I've coined (admittedly a strange if not bizarre and heretical-sounding term), is making sense to me. I've never actually wondered what it means to believe that God is in control. I've never deliberately opened the door of my mind to the question. I think I've lacked the courage. Asking the question might require me to understand the goodness of God in a way that would leave me trembling.

An unexamined question, of course, can never be thoughtfully answered. A happy child's faith works well—until it's tested. Only an examined question will yield answers that can support an adult's faith. For years I have uncritically agreed with a Christian-sounding and apparently God-honoring answer. Is God in control? That's the question. Of course! That's the pat answer. And it is easily embraced by children.

It is time for me to put away childish things and to ask the question:

If God really is in control, why then does He sometimes control things in ways that make no sense to Christians who love Him and who believe that the almighty God loves His people?

Is God in control? The question begs an answer. No one who believes in the God whom the Bible reveals, as I do, would answer no, that God is not in control. Deists would. But I'm not a deist. We Christians confidently and gladly declare that our always present, intimately involved, unfailingly caring, and supremely powerful God remains unthwarted in His control over all that happens. But that comforting truth sometimes fails to provide the comfort we want. It is then we are tempted to believe that a good God will reliably do for us the good we want Him to do. Lies sometimes ease worry more than truth. *eek*

Something is going wrong? It will turn out right. God loves you. Your child is sick? Friends are praying. No worries. God has it covered. Missionaries living in terrorist-occupied territory request prayer for their safety? Your supporting church is praying every day. God is with you. Trust Him. He is in control. You'll be fine. As the old but still loved and catchy familiar spiritual puts it, "He's got the whole world in His hands."

Does He? The wrong gets worse. The child dies. A missionary is killed. Is God in control? I answer yes, but of what? Well, whatever He chooses to control. But what is it God chooses to control? Why didn't He right the wrong, keep the little girl alive, keep all the missionaries safe? He could have. He didn't. Why?

The questions keep coming.

What was God controlling in Paul's life when he was beaten, shipwrecked, imprisoned, and then beheaded? Too often too many Christians answer *everything*, then ignore the confusion their answer raises. Ah, but we must embrace mystery, they say. How could it be less? Our loving and sovereign God controls everything that goes on in our lives, always with our well-being in view. And I respond, tell that to a woman who was raped.

Confusion surrenders to one truth we can agree is true: God does whatever He does for His own glory, to make known the wonders of His infinite goodness, His perfect love, and His unmatched holiness. And because God is who He is, He remains in all moments of time committed to our well-being. But therein lies the rub. Even as we Christians resolutely travel the narrow road to the abundant life that Jesus came to give, our thoughts about what is required in order for us to sing "It is well with my soul" may be quite different from God's.

I find it difficult to declare that God is in control of everything and to imply the obvious corollary, that He is the causative agent behind all that happens. Would that include a toothache that roars with pain at two in the morning when no dentist is available? Does that mean God was responsible for the kidney stone that suddenly made its presence known a few hours before I was scheduled to address a thousand people? Did God control your botched surgery? The onset of your dad's Alzheimer's? The drunk driver who totaled your car and broke your back? The long-prayed-for child who emerged from the womb badly deformed? The teenager over whom you've lost all control?

Or must we conclude that God is in control, but only of some things? With biblical authority, we can trust that God can work something good in all that happens (see Rom. 8:28). But what are the "some things" He controls in order to work the "something good"

113

He promised to bring about? And what is the "greatest good" we can rightly long for that is unerringly on-track through the power of our sovereign God? What is He controlling that we can trust will do us good even when bad things continue?

Those difficult questions are ones that God's loving Spirit is pushing me to ask. Even though His pushing is gentle, it's relentless and not always to my liking. There are days I would prefer to sing "Jesus Loves Me" ten times and then get on with my life.

That option has its appeal. It requires no trembling and offers easy trust. But of this I'm persuaded: only as we wrestle with hard-to-answer questions will confusion pry open the door to deep trust. And only then will we discover tastes of true joy, the joy of recognizing and delighting in the plot of the larger story God is telling, a plot that requires us to tremble before we trust, a plot He fully controls to its eternally dazzling consummation.

~~~

I want now to draw examples from everyday life in our smaller story that help me better understand what Solomon meant when he wrote these words: "I devoted myself to search for understanding and to explore by wisdom everything being done under the sun. I soon discovered that God has dealt a tragic existence to the human race" (Eccles. 1:13).

I think Solomon was anticipating what God later revealed to Paul, that "if our hope in Christ is only for this life, we are more to be pitied than anyone in the world" (1 Cor. 15:19).

Why does the American church so often deny what both Solomon and Paul wrote?

9

Counterfeit Christianity
for Christians

Claiming a Promise God Never Made

In the story of God, things that seem vital to our story fade
into insignificance. And the difficulties of life can be welcomed
as opportunities for Christians to join His story.

Minutes ago (God's timing?) I took a break from writing to
sort through a stack of unopened mail. The second letter I
opened, an official-looking one, informed me that as of yesterday
our health insurance had been canceled. Directions on how to appeal were included, in small print. My wife is scheduled to see her
surgeon tomorrow to follow up on last week's surgery. And I'm on
next week's calendar to endure the next round of expensive tests in
my ongoing battle with cancer.

Our best immediate guess is that a clerical error is responsible for
the unwelcome news. All bills have been paid. We've been in good
standing with our health care plan for more than twenty years. We

will, of course, do all we can to quickly restore coverage. Already on the phone I've listened to long minutes of annoying music while waiting to hear the voice of a live insurance agent.

I will continue to wait. When someone answers, I will talk, and argue if necessary. I will stay on task. That's my job. What is God's? Does He have a part to play in this disturbing mix-up? Is He even involved?

The questions mount. Can my wife and I relax in sure hope that our greatly faithful God, whose mercies are new every morning, will control the outcome of our current muddle in our anxiously desired favor? Prayers have already been requested and offered. Will they be answered? Even though significant health matters are at stake, I have no guarantee from heaven that they will. Surely God is not enjoying our distress. He's no sadist. But He is sovereign. Could He be using our plight for a purpose greater than what would be realized if insurance were restored? Could the purpose He most values be achieved if we're required to scramble for new health coverage?

A Good God

When life assaults us with a problem God has not promised to resolve, it is good, like Habakkuk, to remember promises He has made. Jesus assured us that He would never leave nor forsake us (see Heb. 13:5). God must be nearby, personally aware of the dilemma we've just encountered. Does He care? Is He planning to help? If so, how? I know God loves us. That's not a question still open in my mind. His Son's death has already arranged for our long-term perfect health, no insurance needed. But what about now? What will He do about the health concerns I'm more interested in at this moment?

It's hard to ignore the obvious. Look around. God seems more inclined to *use* suffering than to *relieve* it. A terrorist strikes. We pray. Why? For what? Safety? Another strike happens tomorrow. Many

116

die, in both attacks. And yet, along with fellow Christians, I declare that God is good. But again like many other believers, I struggle to understand the good He is doing. And as I struggle, I tremble, plaintively sighing the prayer so often repeated by Christians when God makes no sense: "I believe; help my unbelief!" (Mark 9:24 ESV). And then the important question again finds its voice to trouble my soul: *What is our good God good for?*

Perhaps I should ask the question differently, more respectfully: *When life throws rocks at us, what is the good news from heaven?* That it was God who threw the rocks for a purpose that only later we will realize was good? That when the rocks come from a fallen world ruled by the prince of evil, God will protect us from serious harm? What exactly does the good news of Christianity assure us we can depend on God to do when trouble and heartbreak come our way? I reply: none of the above.

Is it even conceivable to the modern Christian mind that God delights certainly not in the rocks or the pain they inflict but in the opportunity those rocks provide to align our understanding of the good He promises to do with the good He has in mind?

At some point, life will require every Christian whose head is not buried in the sand of smiling optimism and naïve trust to ask similar questions. Until that point comes, scores of Christians raise their hands in worship every Sunday, praising God for good times with little thought of the good work He does in hard times. Perhaps we should jump ahead on the narrow road and, whether times are pleasant or difficult, ask the unsettling question: God, have You promised to look after my health, my family, my job, my ministry, and my well-being as I understand it? If not, what is the good You promise to do in my life? Uncertainty keeps the question going.

What is it You are doing in the heavenly places where You live that is doing good on earth where I live? You lavish us with spiritual blessings delivered from the realm above the clouds. But what do those blessings have to do with the troubles we face in this world?

You told us to welcome the troubles that upset our comfortable lives, to exploit them as opportunities for great joy (see James 1:2). God, I can think of better news. I wish You would have told me that You would solve my problems. What I'm hearing from You makes me tremble.

So many questions swarm through my mind, none with painless answers. Wrap all the questions together and they come down to this:

What good has God promised to provide in the lives of His followers before we reach heaven?

Modern Christianity has too often come up with a wrong answer. Our spirit of entitlement that demands life work as we think it should feeds our tendency to revise the message of Christianity to better assure us of what we need to enjoy life, what we think we deserve. Without realizing it, we slip into our theology a promise from God that He never made. We then trust God with something He has not pledged to guard.

The teaching of today's counterfeit Christianity for Christians revolves around this one statement of faith: followers of Jesus have warrant from God to assume He will provide whatever we most want to enjoy and to protect us from whatever we most fear to lose.

Put more simply, in many Christian churches and books the cheerful truth is heralded that God will give us what we want and protect us from what we fear. The letter telling me I no longer had health insurance made me immediately aware of what I most wanted: restored coverage. And I know what I most feared: medical bills I would need to pay out of pocket. My pockets are not deep enough.

The lie of counterfeit Christianity is appealing. It *assures me that I have no reason to tremble.* The lie assumes that God's thoughts about what is best for me match mine. And His ways will always please me.

Neither is true.

118

A verse comes to mind that, when read quickly, reinforces the lie. "Delight yourself in the LORD, and he will give you the desires of your heart" (Ps. 37:4 ESV). Is the psalmist telling me to delight in the Lord who will grant every desire that rises in my heart? Or is he saying something quite different? What does he have in mind when he invites us to delight in the Lord *before* we bring Him the desires of our heart? I hear this: as we humbly acknowledge the brilliance of God's thoughts and the beauty of His ways, even when they make no sense to our flawed understanding, we will discover our heart's passionate desire to know Him better and to trust Him for the good He is doing in us and longs to do through us. We have this confidence even when we suffer, when insurance policies are canceled, when a job is lost or a spouse's infidelity is revealed or the air conditioner breaks on summer's hottest day.

Delight in the Lord. Entrust God, as Paul did, to guard our present and eternal well-being in accord with His understanding of well-being. Our eyes will then open, slowly, to recognize what our Spirit-indwelt hearts most desire: *to know God and to surrender to God's ways even when they make no sense to our "this-life-is-all-there-is" way of thinking.*

Joining the Larger Story

The more I delight in the Lord, the more I will desire to know God above all other goods, and I will trust that His indescribable ways are good. But a definite work of God's Spirit is needed to get in touch with my longing to know God and to gladly join the story He is telling. I can't make that happen. I can only open myself to His work and seek it with all my heart.

Christian friends, though well-meaning, too often interfere with the Spirit's work. Friends, pastors, and counselors who have bought into the lie of counterfeit Christianity offer groundless encouragement that builds a crust of false hope around our souls. That lie

119

we have corrupted fallen minds. that need renewing to align with God

prevents us from depending on the deep work God longs to do in our lives. The lie feels good. Either your insurance will be restored or God will provide you with a better, even less expensive policy. Trust God. He "is able to do far more abundantly than all we ask or think, according to the power at work within us" (ESV).

And He is. Those words are in the Bible, in Ephesians 3:20. Again, our entitled spirit interprets the verse to support the lie we want to believe. But Paul is not telling us that God will renew our circumstances to make us comfortable. He is celebrating the truth that God is able to do far more good than our corrupted thoughts lead us to want from Him. And the "power at work within us" (notice *not* "the power at work in our circumstances") transforms us "into a new person" by changing the way we think (Rom. 12:2). As new persons in Christ, we tremble over problems that may not be solved, but we trust that God is doing what our heart most longs for Him to do—to draw us more deeply into His heart.

this is about eternal truths not circumstantial issues in this life.

Is God good? Is He in control? Yes to both questions. It's good news. Because of the finished work of Christ and through the power of the Spirit within us, God promises to change our thoughts and ways, which are far beneath His thoughts and ways. With changed thoughts and trusting ways, we become visible as new persons whether life is working well for us or not. We become "little Christs" (to borrow a term coined by C. S. Lewis) who, like Christ, live to advance God's larger story at any cost to ourselves.

Good news? Not to folks whose thoughts and ways remain un-enlightened. There are Christians who cheerfully assume that on a rainy day God can be trusted to provide a parking space near the shopping mall's entrance. Can He? Of course. Does He? It seems so, sometimes. But He has not promised to grant that blessing. The way God thinks and the way He uses His power hint at a higher purpose than keeping a shopper dry.

When a convenient spot does become available to a Christian, can we be certain God arranged it? Do I dishonor God by lacking firm confidence that it was His doing? A warm thank-you expressed to God for the provision of the space might reveal more proud entitlement than humble gratitude. *Of course God gave it to me. That's what He is supposed to do for His people. Isn't it?*

We close the door on the Spirit's joy rising within us when we trust God to provide the good things of life. Sometimes He provides them, and we give thanks. Sometimes He doesn't. If our joy depends on receiving the blessings we ask God to give us, our joy may disappear. Whether life is comfortable or difficult, the deep joy the Spirit provides when we love like Jesus is always available.

I don't want to be misunderstood. It is right to pray for the blessings we desire and to thank God when they come. But it is wrong to *trust* God to provide them, for two reasons. One, He has not promised to give us the blessings we understandably desire that make life more comfortable. Two, when we confidently trust God to provide convenient parking spots or healing from cancer we aim too low; we set our sights on less joy than God longs for us to know.

Another example. Several weeks ago, my wife felt pressed for time. She was nervously hoping to find a short line at the usually crowded government office where, by the end of the day, she was required to reregister her car. A kind friend, aware of Rachael's pressure, prayed that God would grant her wish.

When Rachael entered the lobby designed to handle dozens of citizens, only one person stood ahead of her in line. Within minutes, served by a friendly, almost chipper clerk, Rachael returned to her now-registered car feeling a bit chipper herself.

Was her good fortune God's doing? Perhaps. Was it right to thank God for the blessing, assuming He provided it? I think so. But it can be maddening to thank God for two hours saved while prayers for an adult son to get saved remain unanswered. And someone more pressed for time than my wife might wait in line for two hours in the same lobby the next day, despite praying for the blessing of a short line.

On a stormy day, another woman might pray for a desirable parking space to clear near the mall entrance. Perhaps she is shopping for a granddaughter's birthday gift. But no space opens. She parks far from the mall. She then runs through heavy rain in heels, trips, falls into a puddle, sprains her ankle, gets soaked, and comes down with pneumonia. Such things happen. And we ask, *What does God choose to control?*

Many Christians answer: everything. Atheists believe there is no God in control of anything. Hard work and good luck account for a life that goes well. Indolence and bad luck explain misfortune. Deists think God does exist but has backed off, letting fickle nature and people's choices run their course.

Glib Christian answers cannot compete with the answers of atheists and deists, not in thinking circles. Our "blessing theology" cannot stand in the light of reason. And faith in "blessing theology" cannot long survive life's happenings. Too much seems random. Lifetime smokers sometimes die of old age. Nonsmokers sometimes contract lung cancer and die early.

But the lie of counterfeit Christianity is still embraced by many Christians. It shields us from trembling, assuring us that our kind and loving God has no greater purpose than to give us what we need for life to work in line with the script we've written for our smaller story and to protect us from whatever trouble we most fear.

It's a tough pill to swallow, but *we must tremble in order to trust*, to trust the way God wants us to trust. Trembling in the presence of a God who makes no sense to our proud understanding of what God should do and what we think He should control opens our soul, sometimes in desperation, to trust that His thoughts are wise and His ways are good. We then learn what it means to rest as we trust that God, in unthwarted sovereignty, is doing the good we most value, in us and through us, even when rocks are hurled into our lives.

It is then we see the good in the story God is telling. We glimpse a vision of who we're becoming: stable, strong, sensitive disciples of Jesus who see a beauty in the community of God that nothing in nature can match. We become people who "count it all joy" when trials come (James 1:2 ESV). I'm not yet there. But like a child on Christmas Eve, I'm looking forward to the morning.

Three phases of my journey have brought me to where I find myself now, in a fourth place where I can believe that what I've felt to be impossible is now possible: *I could learn to deeply trust the God who sometimes makes no sense.* A review of those three phases I've passed through might shed light on one man's narrow-road journey to life.

10

A Long Journey
toward an Elusive Goal

> Our stories form us. To some degree, they deform us. Even
> the story of a happy childhood forms us in ways that need re-
> forming. God's good news slowly forms us to trust God's love
> as we tremble in this world until we live without trembling in
> a world made new.

As a young Christian, saved by Christ from sin's penalty at age
eight, the questions I'm asking now, more than a half cen-
tury later, never crossed my mind. Life was good. I was living the
American dream. I enjoyed a good family, a warm home, school
success, and summers on the ball field with plenty of friends. Simple
trust in a good God grounded in untested faith came easily. God was
good. The evidence? Life was good. Phase One was underway: *no
trembling. Only trust.*

Phase One

I was raised by lovingly attentive and justly strict parents, both strong Christians. From my earliest days of conscious awareness to my midteen years, I effortlessly believed not only that there was a God but that He was good, kind, supportive, and generous. When I learned that, thanks to Jesus, I could refer to His Father as my Father, I assumed He would look out for me the way my earthly father did. Occasional but always deserved spankings never administered in anger were surrounded by good times with Dad; playing tennis, watching Red Skelton together on our ten-inch black-and-white television every Tuesday night, and observing how seriously he lived his faith.

I had no reason to doubt my father's goodness. Whatever he could control, he controlled with my well-being in view. Would my heavenly Father do less? I knew how good fathers treated their children. I was God's son. Good times would continue.

Never in Sunday school or Christian camp or youth group did I hear any mention of hard times in a Christian's life. Why would there be? God would protect me from them. He was good. My understanding of the word *good* was firmly in place. The idea that hard times could further God's good purpose never occurred to me.

God was good. But He was also holy. I learned a dozen rules by which a Christian should live, from youth leaders and Sunday preachers. I picked up the concept that if I obeyed the rules, God would keep my life running smoothly. Don't smoke. Don't drink. Don't cheat. Don't lie. Don't have sex before marriage. Keep the rules and life works. I was willing to control my unholy impulses. The deal seemed fair.

I got it. The journey with God was a quid pro quo arrangement. I do good; God treats me good. A way was opened for me to get from God what I wanted. In Sunday school I had heard that Jesus invited thirsty people to come to Him. His words were recorded in John 7:37. I knew I was thirsty for the good things of life. I often came to Jesus in prayer, waving my wish list before a divine Santa

Claus, believing His jolly voice, though unheard, was promising to deliver everything on the list.

I was aware of no desire for anything more. Thirsty for God's *presence*? No, I wanted His *presents*. He wanted to bless me. That was His job. Mine was to keep the rules. Apostate Israelite thinking

The arrangement worked well, for a while. I did my best to be a good son to God. Most often, He proved Himself to be a good Father. Christianity as I then understood it was a convenient religion. A good God was in control of my life and doing a good job. *I wonder how many Christians never leave Phase One.*

Phase Two

Teen years blended into the twenties. Tasting the looming responsibilities of adulthood made me aware of new challenges and new questions. Two topped the list, both unnerving. Phase Two began.

Most of my high school and college friends (both school and college were secular institutions) were not Christians. To them, Jesus, if they gave Him any thought, was either a failed messiah or a good teacher. They had not been raised in Christian homes. That got me thinking. Maybe their lack of faith was more inherited than chosen. Did that mean that my faith was merely an inheritance from Christian parents? The possibility troubled me.

I never chose to speak the English language. With no intent to do so, I learned English in my English-speaking home. Was I a professing Christian for no better reason than that I was born into a Christian home, favorably exposed to no competing religion or worldview? Had I been raised by Orthodox Jewish parents, would I now be waiting for the true messiah to come?

I was content with speaking an unchosen language. English served me well in my family, friendships, school, and community. Was I content with continuing to embrace an unchosen faith?

127

That was the first question that led me out of Phase One with its easy faith. A second one proved more unsettling. Important decisions had to be made. Whom to marry? What career to pursue? I met Rachael when we were both ten. In our teen years we dated a few others but always drifted back together. Was it romance? Or convenience? Maybe a comfortable habit? However a teenager knows such things, I knew I loved Rachael. Was it true love? More importantly, was it God's will? I sensed no direction from heaven. I remember asking where God was. He seemed absent.

Another decision was required. When I was a college senior, a prestigious medical school solicited my enrollment with the promise of financial assistance. But I had majored in psychology, mostly because hypnosis fascinated me and mental illness, especially schizophrenia, intrigued me. I felt more interest in understanding psychological disorders than physical disease. Was that God's leading? I didn't know. Again I asked where God was. I heard nothing from Him to help guide me in career plans.

Moving from teen years into my twenties, I felt the temptation to break some of God's rules grow strong. Feelings of insecurity and fear of inadequacy gathered unfamiliar strength. Shouldn't God provide the divine power needed to resist temptation and the divine presence to heal my emotional struggles and wounds? He provided neither. At least that's how it seemed to me. I knew God promised to provide "the way of escape" (1 Cor. 10:13 ESV) from sin's seductive power, but so often in the moment of temptation the way seemed blocked. Prayer seemed pointless. Church did little more than remind me of the rules I was breaking. My Phase One faith was wobbling. God was on trial. As the prosecuting attorney I asked the jury, *What good is God?* I heard nothing. The question continued to reverberate in the courtroom of my mind. I couldn't come up with an answer. I didn't know.

I encountered a God who made no sense to me. I had no compelling interest in joining the story He was telling. Unchosen faith was not serving me well. Had God abandoned me? Why wasn't He delivering what I thought Christianity promised to give? Did God even exist? If so, what was He good for?

The questions assaulted me. But I was reluctant to seriously engage them. They might lead me to abandon the God who had seemed to abandon me. Given my background, with its teaching on heaven and hell, I chose a middle ground of compromise. The fear of eternal misery kept me in the fold.

I thought I could make my way as a card-carrying Christian while setting my sights on no higher goal than adding the letters PhD after my name on a business card. Perhaps psychology could provide the insight I needed to move happily and successfully through life. I envisioned a well-paid career as a therapist, nodding to Christian thinking as I freed others from neurotic disorders, character flaws, and relational tangles, depending mostly on therapeutic theory and technique, with perhaps an occasional prayer.

But a fly found its way into my ointment. Five years of doctoral training in clinical psychology proved disillusioning. I felt strangely bothered when it became apparent that secular psychology and biblical Christianity mixed about as well as oil and water. From Freud to Skinner and beyond, psychologists typically had no interest in learning God's thoughts about life or in studying God's ways of dealing with people. A few of my professors openly scoffed at the amusing notion that Christianity had anything to say about restoring people to a truly good life, to help them become more human. Psychotherapy was humanity's best hope.

For reasons I now attribute to the Holy Spirit, I was unable to push God into the periphery of irrelevance. The hunch remained. Maybe God did exist as the lovingly good and powerful God I once naïvely believed Him to be. What was I to do? I couldn't deny that psychology had something to contribute to my thinking. Was I to integrate psychology with Christianity? Was it even possible?

A mind opened by confusion became God's opportunity. I had been wandering in Phase Two: *No trust. Only trembling.* Through what I can now recognize as providence, Phase Two ended during one long night. Phase Three began.

Phase Three

I was in my late twenties, a successfully practicing psychologist. Still unsettled, one early sleepless morning, hours before dawn, I was reading *The God Who Is There*, written by noted Christian thinker Francis Schaeffer. Without warning a complicated idea formed in my mind, with clarity. It went something like this:

If there really is a God, and if the God who is there is the infinite and personal God that Schaeffer sees revealed in the Bible, then it would be reasonable to assume that His "above time" thoughts and ways would make no sense to our "time bound" ways of thinking. Psychological theory, empirical research, and philosophy's speculation, each done with finite understanding, can never become aware of the story an infinite God is telling.

And then it hit me: *Revelation is required.* Without revelation from God, the mystery of His thoughts and ways will forever remain unentered and unknown. And without God's Spirit opening souls of fallen humans to make them aware of their thirst for God, the mystery will never be attractive. To whatever degree God's thoughts and ways were seen, human pride would find them of no value. They wouldn't make sense.

With a weight that crushed my pride (I wish I could say completely) and with a hope that lifted me to new heights (I wish I could report I've stayed there ever since), a single truth exploded into life: *God has spoken!* He has revealed Himself to us. He has made known the larger story that He scripted and is now telling, the story unfolding above the sun. And He has invited us and made it possible for us to celebrate the goodness of the story, a good-

our vision has to be set higher → set your mind on the things above where christ is seated col

ness that looks bad to people who see only what is visible below the sun.

On that morning, the Bible became important to me in a measure I had never before appreciated. I walked into Phase Three. The door opened to the promised land of *inspired trust. Muted trembling.* Years passed, four decades of them, before I understood that yet another phase, the most dangerous and frightening of them all, would be required in my pursuit of the elusive goal. More about that later.

I committed myself to exploring a Christianity that could only come alive with liberating truth through a lifelong study of the Bible. A variety of Bible translations, Hebrew and Greek lexicons, and scholarly commentaries on every one of God's sixty-six love letters soon found their way onto my bookshelves. I was zealous after knowledge, not the puffing-up kind but rather knowledge that would change me and satisfy my mind and soul.

The shift into Phase Three was dramatic. Phase One, already left behind, was now buried deep. No more comfortably believing what a good Christian boy raised in a good Christian home was supposed to believe. No more inherited Christianity. Phase Two was similarly discarded. No more casually carrying the Christian card solely to avoid hell in the next life while I looked to psychology to make life work in this one, according to my tastes. I was eager to depend on the Bible and the Spirit's enlightenment to come up with a settled understanding of how people could live the abundant life Jesus promised to His followers as they lived not of the world but in the world. I suspected that my earlier understanding of the good that God intended to do for us, in us, and through us would require revision, likely revolutionary revision. Maybe He had something better to offer than this-world blessings.

I studied the Bible as best I could. I continued to read widely in psychology and a little in philosophy; I made time to enjoy classical literature, all the way from Augustine to Dickens. I hoped that a deepening understanding of secular thought would encourage more careful biblical thinking, perhaps alerting me to when my developing views crossed boundaries set by an orthodox Christian worldview. Among others, Dostoyevsky (particularly his classic *Crime and Punishment*), Kierkegaard, Pascal, C. S. Lewis, and J. I. Packer led me into theological depths my own limited capacities wouldn't allow me to reach.

I enjoyed flesh-fueling success from my thirties into my sixties. People read the books I wrote. Clients came to my counseling office. Many folks listened to me in the conferences and seminars I led. Students enrolled in the classes I taught. And yet I felt tortured in my soul, always struggling to be open to God's deepest work in me and always worried that I wasn't. The Spirit was preparing me for Phase Four.

I recognized that too often I was with people to prove I could help them, to nourish my sense of adequacy. Too little I was with people to enjoy them, to celebrate them as souls designed for greatness, not in their eyes or the world's but in God's. In subtle, hard to recognize, but vaguely felt ways, I managed people more than encountering them.] ouch

Phase Three was a long season of grappling with unresolved confusion that prompted me to trust God for the wisdom I needed to bring biblical truth to hurting people that would set them free. But the freedom I unknowingly valued most was the freedom to satisfy lesser thirsts, not the supreme thirst to trust God when He makes no sense. I had yet to understand the need to tremble before we trust. Oh, I trembled. But I trusted God to remove its cause.

Phase Four

God's Spirit was not content to leave me where I had camped on my journey toward God, toward the God who would give me enough blessings to let me rest in His presence, no longer tortured by confusion and with no reason to tremble. God had a different plan. He intended to lead me toward the elusive goal of confidently, even joyfully, trusting God when what He allowed to go on in my life would make me tremble in sorrow, uncertainty, and confusion.

He is now using unhealed cancer, advancing age and all that comes with it, and soul weariness to incline me to reflect on my journey thus far:

- Phase One, from my earliest years to midteens, the brief era of *pleasant Christianity* made possible by naïve trust. No trembling required; only trust, the immature variety.
- Phase Two, the decade of late teens to late twenties, a season of *unsettled Christianity*. God wouldn't deliver what I thought He should give me. His stubbornness drove me to no trust, really angry distrust, and self-focused trembling over confusion.
- Phase Three, my four-decade journey of *blessed Christianity*, blessings that prevented the torture I felt from undoing me. Enough blessings to allow me to trust God for continued blessings, a trust that muted my trembling.

Remember the sentence that appeared early in chapter 8: "Three somewhat distinct phases of my journey through life as a hopefully forming Christian, phases I will describe in chapter 10, have brought me to where I find myself today, in what I experience as a hard place but feel mostly confident is a good one." I have entered Phase Four.

I am coming to grips with the intimidating truth that God's thoughts and ways are far above mine. Isn't the abundant life that Jesus promised to provide for His followers an abundance of blessings that keep us happy, never having to wrestle with fear or disappointment? It finally dawned on me with unsettling power that my understanding of what is good did not match God's. My understanding of the good that my God should provide had been disastrously shaped by my proud, blind self-centeredness as I lived in a fallen world committed to feeling full *now*. For so long my flawed thinking had seemed so reasonable, unworthy of being questioned, in need of no correction.

Not only my thinking was defective. I also realized my ways of handling good times and bad did not align with God's ways of dealing with all that I saw as right in the world and all that I saw as wrong. The truth of Isaiah 55:8, that God's thoughts about life and His ways of involving Himself with our lives are immeasurably above mine, hit me with thundering power that, predictably, left me thunderstruck. I had willfully resisted a humble look at the thoughts and ways of God. I wanted a God who would cooperate with my understanding of what was best for me. I didn't want to hear a story told by God that would leave me trembling.

In Part 3, I want to explore what it means and what it takes to value the kind of trust that develops when we tremble before a God who makes no sense. Trembling in the presence of our inscrutable God frees us to rely on the good and loving God whose thoughts and ways are far above ours, to trust Him—for what?

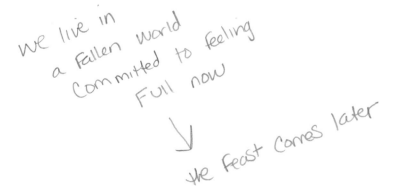

we live in a Fallen world Committed to feeling Full now

the Feast comes later

PART 3

_____ ⌇ _____

When God's Ways
Make No Sense

*Trust in God's Unthwarted
Sovereignty*

There are three responses when God's ways make no sense to us: resist and run, distort and deny, tremble and trust. Only one is blameless. Only one leads to joy. Part 1 illustrated each response in the lives of three men: Jonah, Saul, and Habakkuk. In Part 2, focusing on Habakkuk's response, I explored what it means and why it is necessary to tremble in the presence of a God who so often makes no sense to our way of thinking.

Still in Part 2, I struggled with my belief that God is in full control and suggested that He is in full control of the larger story He is telling, a hard-to-see story of divine goodness and love that, in moments, even seasons, can appear to be a story of pointless hardships. As we live with our eyes fixed on our smaller story, God can sometimes come across to us as a hands-off God, a God who capriciously withholds His goodness and who seems to back away when we need Him most.

In Part 3, I tackle two challenges.

One, I try to understand a kind of trust that seems foreign to most of us in today's feel-good, don't-tremble Christian culture. It's a trust exhibited in the greatest saints of history and in a few today, all martyrs for the cause of Christ. These are men and women who maintained a firm, glad trust in God's goodness, even as God did nothing to save them from severe trials, including burning at the stake for the crime of following Jesus. It is that kind of trust that God's Spirit makes available to you and me, the least of saints, whether we face martyrdom in painful death or in painful life.

Two, I wonder what things our good and gentle God must do (some that in the moment will seem neither good nor gentle) to provide the soil in which trembling is revealed to be a seed that sprouts into the beautiful flower of Habakkuk-like trust.

With this brief review of Parts 1 and 2 and an even briefer preview of Part 3, let me now enter into a discussion of the meaning of this exhortation:

When God's ways make no sense,
trust in
God's unthwarted sovereignty.

11

The High Calling to Trust

Is It Too High?

> For the earnestly and patiently God-seeking Christian, life will
> bring us to the desirable necessity of absolute surrender.

I felt blocked as I prayed this morning. A wall of indifference rose up between my heart and God. I lost interest in speaking with Him. Maybe the wall had more to do with frustration. I couldn't see the point of spending time praying.

I unexpectedly awoke from a sound sleep a little before 3:00 a.m. The names and faces of two close, committed Christian friends appeared in my mind. My immediate reflexive thought felt alive: *God's Spirit is prompting me to pray for them.*

Both friends are enduring a rough season. Both are weighed down with troubling disappointment. One recently underwent delicate surgery performed by a top specialist. The surgery did not produce the eagerly desired and fervently prayed-for result, a result that would have significantly improved her quality of life. The other, a gifted and seminary-trained Bible teacher, is stuck in a dead-end job. Despite

137

several years of consistent prayer for work that he longs to do, dozens of sent-out résumés have turned up no opportunities.

Wide awake and now sitting up in bed, I thought about what these two friends were going through. Compassion seemed to flow from deep places within me. Surely God must be feeling far more compassion than I was capable of. Strangely, as I began to pray, I remembered Pascal's comment that prayer gives us the dignity of causality. We can make a difference in someone's life. With a quiet surge of excited hope, I prayed that the desired result of surgery would suddenly occur and miraculously surprise my friend. Amen. Let it be so.

The excitement quickly faded. In less than a minute, I could feel the energy supporting my prayer drain out of me. Raw faith (perhaps naïve faith?) was needed to continue. It wasn't there. To myself, I muttered, "What's the point?" It wasn't a question looking for an answer. It was a statement of resignation.

Still in the early hours of morning, my thoughts turned to my underemployed friend, a godly man who experiences dark seasons of feeling abandoned by God. I could feel an angrily compelling desire rising up in me, more like a demand, to see God open the door to a ministry that would release my friend to live the calling he remains convinced came from God. Of course, God could arrange for such an opportunity. Why wouldn't He?

So I prayed, with longing, for my friend to be suitably employed. Again, in less than a minute, the longing disappeared in a fog of cynicism. With trust in God's goodness, Jesus prayed "Not My will but Thine be done." My prayer took a different form: "Why isn't Your will the same as mine?"

I stopped praying.

That was wrong of me to do. I know the story Jesus told to His impatient disciples in Luke 18:1–8, the one about a widow who didn't stop praying. Despite no response, she persisted in her plea for justice to an uncaring judge. Persistence paid off. She got what she asked for. Is Jesus telling us that persistent prayers will always be answered? Or are we to learn that prayer without ceasing reflects trust in God's goodness and has value in His eyes whether answers come or not?

I felt a hint of conviction: whatever else He was saying, Jesus was making a simple point, that His followers "should always pray and never give up" (Luke 18:1). He wanted us to know that we pray to a compassionate Father, not to an uncaring judge. I believe that. But the conviction to keep pleading with God was weak. I didn't keep praying. I gave up.

I slumped back onto my pillow, my mind a tangle of frustration and confusion. *What does it mean to trust God?* Of course, He is worthy of my confidence in His love and goodness. The cross leaves no room for doubt. I should trust Him. I should honor the high calling to trust that God will keep His promise to always do me good. Speaking about Israel, God said this: "I will never stop doing good for them. . . . I will find joy doing good for them" (Jer. 32:40–41). In another place, this time speaking directly to Israel, God said "I know the plans I have for you. . . . They are plans for good and not for disaster, to give you a future and a hope" (29:11). I assume that promise holds true for God's people today.

Faith-Supported Confidence

I should trust God. And I want to trust God. I know He is good. But what good can I pray, and trust God to do, for someone after failed surgery or during continued unsatisfying employment?

Is there a good I can pray for with confidence
that it will be provided by God?

With these questions assaulting me, I gave up on sleep, climbed out of bed, dressed, and reached for my Bible. I turned to Psalm 25, where David tells us how he prayed when faced with trouble. "To you, O LORD, I lift up my soul." Why? For what? "O my God, in you I trust" (Ps. 25:1, 2 ESV). *David, what were you trusting God to do?* I wanted to know. I wasn't sure.

I continued reading. David prayed that he wouldn't "be put to shame" and that his enemies would not "exult over" him. Was David asking to never be embarrassed over a faith that proved to be false, to never let his enemies be justified in mocking his confidence in God's goodness? In verse 5, he declared, "for you I wait all day long." Why the long wait? The high calling of God to trust Him: I wanted to know what it was. In my understanding, it seemed too high. How was I to trust God that the next test would reveal my cancer was healed? That may not be the good God promised to give.

I then flipped over a few pages to Psalm 37 to read the familiar words of David where he shifts the focus from *his* trust to encouraging *us* to trust God. His exhortation is direct: "Trust in the LORD, and do good. . . . Delight yourself in the LORD, and he will give you the desires of your heart" (37:3–4 ESV). Another hint of conviction: *Do I delight in the Lord? Do I like Him only when He does what I want Him to do?*

In this psalm, I hear David assuring me that God will grant whatever desires are alive in my heart that, when granted, will advance what God most wants to bring about. Wouldn't a loving God want to bring about good health in a godly woman and a kingdom-advancing job for a godly man trained to pastor? If not, why not? I am aware of the usual understanding of these verses, and I agree with it: that delighting in the Lord—in other words, surrendering to the effect of His thoughts and ways even when they make no sense—will shape our desires into those He most longs to satisfy. Again I ask: What yearning does God most long to satisfy that I could confidently desire? We delight in the Lord when we trust what He does because He is powerfully good and infinitely loving.

I suppose most Christians respond positively to teaching that instructs us to delight in the Lord, trust Him to do us good, then pray for what we want, believing God intends to give us an abundant life. And He does. But it's hard for us to conceive of an abundant life that is not abundant in what we are aware we most want. I fear, however, that too often we hear solid biblical teaching—God loves us and has a wonderful plan for our lives—and warmly receive it as sweet truth. And it is that. But truth that is sweet is not always experienced as pleasant. The surgery fails to heal. No opportunity for the job we want presents itself. But we delight in our prayer-answering God. We know He loves us. The truth of His loving goodness is sweet to our ears—until trouble comes. We pray for an abundance of blessings, thinking that the good things of life provide the richest satisfaction. Instead, an abundance of difficulties comes.

Do we delight in the God of love who is doing us as much good when life is difficult as when it is untroubled? Could He be doing us more good when trials come? If so, what is the better good? Truth that we easily receive as sweet must be embraced as true truth, even when we see little evidence of God's goodness during bad times.

A third close friend clung to the truth of Psalm 37 when he was diagnosed with terminal cancer. He resolved to delight in God as His loving Father and present Lord, to trust God and do good while he pleaded with God to give him the desires of his heart. I knew my friend well. He desired to go home and see Jesus, but he also longed to live, as much if not more for his wife and children as for himself. I asked him how often he thought about heaven. His answer was one I did not expect. "Not much. I want to keep my focus on the life I'm now living."

Hundreds of people whose lives he had touched prayed for a miraculous cure as he endured extensive and not always pleasant treatment. Within a few months of increasing weakness and discomfort, he died. Was God good to him? Did God grant the desires of my friend's heart? Was his strongest God-shaped desire to die? Questions. More questions. Always questions, questions that we never really ask when life is moving along nicely. These questions concentrated themselves in my mind during that long morning.

Does the high calling of God oblige us to trust Him to do a good work—maybe His best work—when we're enduring hard times? Can we receive the true truth that God is, in fact, doing something good in us and for us during the consequences we live with after a failed surgery, during a frustrating job with no visible hope for a better one, during a season of impending death—and can we receive it as sweet truth?

Bitter and Sweet

I wonder how often we raise our arms during a rousing worship service of praise, then lower them to listen to a pastor tell us that God's good story is unfolding through every trouble that comes our way. Do we hear his message as truth that tastes sweet until it's tested? What happens then?

God told Ezekiel, "Open your mouth, and eat what I give you." A hand then reached out to the prophet, holding a scroll. When the scroll was unrolled, Ezekiel saw that "both sides were covered with funeral songs, words of sorrow, and pronouncements of doom" (Ezek. 2:8, 10). God's calling to Ezekiel to trust Him was high. "Fill your stomach with this," God ordered (3:3). The obedient prophet then ate the scroll on which funeral songs, words of sorrow, and pronouncements of doom were written. Perhaps because he knew these harsh words came from a good God, the words "tasted as sweet as honey" in Ezekiel's mouth (v. 3). Had God said nothing more, and had Ezekiel gone out for coffee with friends, I suppose the sweet taste might not have turned sour.

But then God told Ezekiel, "Son of man, let all my words sink deep into your own head first. Listen to them carefully for yourself. Then go to your people in exile and say to them, 'This is what the sovereign LORD says!' Do this whether they listen to you or not" (vv. 10–11). Perhaps Ezekiel felt like pastors who refuse to flinch from preaching the whole counsel of God, including the truth that

God does not promise to protect His children from all trouble. The sweet taste turned bitter for Ezekiel. After hearing God's marching orders, Ezekiel tells us that "The Spirit lifted me up and took me away. I went in bitterness and turmoil, but the LORD's hold on me was strong" (v. 14).

The deeply good and therefore sweet truth of all God's thoughts and ways that control His sovereign movement in our lives, movement that sometimes makes no sense to our comfort-entitled way of thinking, can only become true truth that sustains us when life gets hard. Does God call us then to turn to Him in trust, with confidence in His unfailing love as the God who "did not spare His own Son" in His plan to do us good and who therefore is sure to "also with him graciously give us all things" (Rom. 8:32 ESV)? Are we to trust that no matter the unexpected trouble we experience, His hold on us will be strong, a hold that will keep us faithful when the truth of His plan tastes bitter?

Generations after Ezekiel, another scroll was given to a man of God by an angel of God. On this scroll was written that the city of God on earth would be devastated. The apostle John took the scroll, a small one, and ate it. His experience matched Ezekiel's. "It was sweet in my mouth, but when I swallowed it, it turned sour in my stomach" (Rev. 10:10). He, too, was commanded to deliver the distressing message to God's people.

Throughout the New Testament, with no exceptions, we hear a message that is sweet because it comes from our loving, saving, tender God. But parts of the message are bitter, more about funeral songs, words of sorrow, and pronouncements of doom than good times ahead. Without realizing what we're doing, valuing our comfortable life, we receive the hard news into our mouths then spit it out when we close our Bibles, leave church, join friends for Sunday lunch, then go home to watch a ball game.

Listen to the message that our comfort-craving Christian culture prefers to spit out:

- "For this world is not our permanent home; we are looking forward to a home yet to come" (Heb. 13:14).
- "Dear friends, don't be surprised at the fiery trials you are going through, as if something strange were happening to you. Instead, be very glad—for these trials make you partners with Christ in his suffering, so that you will have the wonderful joy of seeing his glory when it is revealed to all the world" (1 Pet. 4:12–13).
- "You should know this, Timothy, that in the last days there will be very difficult times" (2 Tim. 3:1).
- "Here on earth you will have many trials and sorrows" (John 16:33).
- "With the strength God gives you, be ready to suffer with me for the sake of the Good News" (2 Tim. 1:8).
- "We must suffer many hardships to enter the Kingdom of God" (Acts 14:22).

Not only failed surgeries, frustrating jobs, and impending death but also tension in churches, unrelenting temptations, broken families, betraying friends, anxious feelings, and a host of other struggles will plague our lives. The high call to trust involves the call to endure. Consider a brief sample of the many verses that urge us to persevere through trial, not to expect deliverance:

- "Here is a call for the endurance of the saints," issued in the expectation of terrible suffering (Rev. 14:12 ESV).
- "Patient endurance is what you need now" (Heb. 10:36).
- "Put on every piece of God's armor so you will be able to resist the enemy in the time of evil" (Eph. 6:13).

Trouble is inevitable. Endurance is necessary. Our high call from God is to trust Him and to trust His heart, a heart filled with love.

Nothing can happen to us or in us that He cannot work together for our good. Is the call too high? Am I to delight in God not only when He showers me with blessings but also when I suffer? Do we even like the story God is telling? Have we distorted His plot into one that better fits our expectation of what a good God should do with all His power? And when troubles come, do we hear the high calling to trust His love no matter what further troubles come our way? Again I ask, is the call too high? Or will honoring the call to trust God in every circumstance of life and in any condition of soul lead us to become the people we most long to be? *What is the path to that kind of trust?* The question needs an answer.

12

In God We Trust

For the Good He Gives or the Good We Want?

> God longs to give us what our Spirit-indwelt hearts most want,
> but only hors d'oeuvres now—the banquet later. The question
> then arises: Are we aware of what we were created to most enjoy?

In a historical piece in the newspaper, I recently read that when
President John F. Kennedy was assassinated in the prime of his
successful life, his wife Jackie, a devout Catholic, trembled in tears
of bewilderment and anguish as she asked a friend, "How could a
loving God allow such a terrible thing to happen?" Her husband's
untimely death, heartbreaking to so many, made no sense to her
understanding of who God is and what He's about.

I suspect that beneath that one tormenting question, two others
were rummaging somewhere in her mind: Is God really in control of
all that happens in this world? And if He is, assuming He exists, how
can anyone believe He is the God of love He claims to be? Whether
or not she was aware of it at the time, Mrs. Kennedy was struggling
with what it means to call God sovereign. More about that later.

We're not so different from this grieving widow. "In God We Trust," America's obscured but national slogan, is for many who repeat it a lackadaisical hope that God would do a better job of running the world. Perhaps an occasional prayer will win His co-operation in arranging things to our liking.

Christians, of course, put more stock in the message of the slogan. And yet, in our entitled "It's all about me" culture, we evangelicals credulously trust God—our heavenly Father, our crucified Lord, and our indwelling Holy Spirit—to prevent tragedy in our grace-favored lives and to bless us with enough creature comforts for us to enjoy getting up in the morning. It is right to pray for both. But we have the right to neither, and victory in the Christian life is not defined by these.

Sometimes God blesses us as we wish. Sometimes He doesn't. Sometimes a loved one lives in good health to a ripe old age when even healthy folks are bound to die. And the bereaved hurt, but we sincerely (and properly) thank our gracious God that the one we loved lived a long and happy life. We exit the memorial service with good memories, sad but grateful.

Sometimes the one we love most dies before death should claim anyone. Was the loving, sovereign God in whom we trust on duty then? However life turns hard, when it happens on God's watch, as it always does, it's difficult to not wonder if God is fickle, insensitively unpredictable, perhaps looking after higher priorities than our protection and happiness. God seems prone to making what we can only think of as erratic decisions with little or no thought given to the well-being of those He claims to love.

As Christians, worshipers of God, we don't want to fall into such sacrilege. But the data supporting that wrong thinking can be uncomfortably compelling. A mature Christian woman in her fifties whose life has bounced from one gut-wrenching disaster to another recently told me, "If God really is sovereignly in control of everything, I sometimes think He should be found guilty on charges of abuse."

The only way to avoid buying into such God-dishonoring thinking is to accept a pride-humbling, brokenness-producing truth that turns much of modern Christianity on its head:

God's understanding of what it means to love us is radically different from ours; and more, it is repugnant to our fallen vision of how God should demonstrate His love for us.

And yet He issues the high calling to trust His love, to believe that in every moment of our lives, pleasant moments and unbearable ones, God is pouring His faithful love "into our hearts" (Rom. 5:5 ESV). A Southern gospel song captures our call from God pretty well: "When you can't trace His hand, trust His heart."[1] More easily sung than lived.

Since childhood, I've been plagued by an unholy temptation to think and to do what no Christian should think or do; a flesh-driven urge that doesn't fit well in a Christian's life. It's a poor fit in mine. And I'm regretfully confident that some equally shame-worthy desire lies in every Christian still living.

The apostle John, I think, would agree. As an old man who for three years witnessed the purity in the heart of Jesus made visible in His life and who saw the impurity in his own heart and in the hearts of the many Christians he knew, John wrote these words in a letter to several churches: "If we claim to have no sin, we are only fooling ourselves and not living in the truth" (1 John 1:8). Spiritual cancer is alive in every Christian. Malignant urges plague the best of us.

Like mine, many such urges only grow stronger and more insatiable with passing years. I hate mine. I hate its seemingly intractable power that in moments compels me to love it, to love the opportunity the urge, if indulged, provides for a kind of consuming pleasure that our holy God won't provide.

Neither prayers begging God to diminish the temptation's strength to a more manageable level nor pleas for Him to develop in me the mettle to withstand its coercive force have been answered. Why? Is there another path to the victory I so desire? God has promised to be my helper in time of need, my "refuge and strength, a very present help in trouble" (Ps. 46:1 ESV). Why, then, when I cry to Him for help as temptation presses me to yield, do I sometimes sense His absence? He can't be indifferent. And yet too often He seems far away, removed from my troubles, irrelevant to my need.

Difficult Obedience

Perhaps C. S. Lewis has something to say to Christians who experience God as remote. In *The Screwtape Letters*, Lewis suggests that God's thoughts and ways confound not only Christians who seek Him but also devils who hate Him. In the book, Uncle Screwtape, a senior demon assigned to mentor his nephew, junior demon Wormwood, counsels Wormwood on how to keep a human from trusting God, hell's Enemy. He writes:

> You must have often wondered why the Enemy does not make more use of His power to be sensibly present to human souls in any degree He chooses and at any moment. . . . He leaves the creature to stand up on its own legs—to carry out from the will alone duties which have lost all relish.

Duties such as praying? Screwtape goes on:

> It is during such trough periods, much more than during peak periods, that it is growing into the sort of creature He wants it to be. Hence the prayers offered in the state of dryness are those which please Him best.[2]

Could that be true? One would think that grateful prayers of thanksgiving rising to God during peak periods of blessing would most delight Him. If Screwtape is aware of something true, then determined prayers of resolute trust when our souls are dry provide more delight for God and do something better in us than prayers of thanks for enjoyed good times.

When I see no point in asking God to restore health in a sick friend, to provide a fulfilling job for a discouraged friend, or to pray for weakened temptation for my struggling self; if I fail to pray *with trust that God is doing good even when prayers are not answered*, I miss the opportunity to become more of the sort of creature God wants me to be.

Screwtape then adds this sentence, one that I find especially convicting:

> Our cause is never more in danger than when a human no longer desiring, but still intending, to do our Enemy's will, looks round upon a universe from which every trace of Him seems to have vanished, and asks why he has been forsaken, *and still obeys*.[3]

But such obedience, choosing to trust God's love when "every trace" of His goodness seems to have vanished, is not easy. And yet we're commanded to imitate Jesus in His suffering when He did exactly that, during the three hours when He felt utterly abandoned by His Father. It was then that "God was in Christ, reconciling the world to himself" (2 Cor. 5:19). Imagine what God's Spirit could be doing in us if we trusted His love in our worst moments.

Faith, of course, is required to activate our will, to kick it into motion toward a good end. Without faith, it is simply impossible to please Him (see Heb. 11:6). It follows that obedience without faith in God's goodness, obedience that is designed to win "deserved" blessings from God, does not please God. But with faith, even with faith the size of a tiny mustard seed, nothing would be impossible (see Matt. 17:20–21). It's clear, however, that we cannot work up real faith on our own. Paul told us that faith is a gift from God (see

Eph. 2:8). Does God sometimes withhold that gift, for a season of a length He determines, leaving us unable to trust His love? Does our consequent failure somehow work for our good?

It seems so. Troubles harass Christians as much as they do non-Christians—sometimes more. There are times we simply cannot find it in us to confidently trust His loving intentions. Perhaps that is why Augustine prayed the famous prayer, "Command what you wish, but give what you command."[4] Maybe that's the prayer we should pray when we experience

> *troubles without*, such as a loved one's unexpected and untimely death, a failed surgery, long-term underemployment or unemployment with all the financial pressures that follow, severe marital tension and perhaps divorce, children who break their parents' hearts, disappointing friends, an ex-spouse who delights to hassle their former mate, or
>
> *troubles within*, such as temptation to do evil, wounds from abuse that neither prayer nor counseling heals, felt distance from God when His presence feels most needed, unbearable loneliness, no clear guidance from heaven when a critical decision must be made, migraines that won't quit, a scary diagnosis from the doctor, worry over signs of developing Alzheimer's.

It's puzzling. The list of troubles that batter God's well-loved children is long. Each one God could prevent or untangle. Why doesn't He? Again the familiar question screams for an answer: *What good is God?*

I repeat the question, and underline the difficulties that require committed Christians to at least ask it, for one reason: *Christians whose lives are replete with blessings typically don't bother even to think about these things.* They therefore risk becoming lukewarm

Christians, children of God who never discover the unsought good that their Father most longs to do in their lives, the best good that can only be done in the hard times they live to avoid.

There is a second reason to raise the question again. When suffering breaks into the comfort-seeking life of a Christian, as inevitably it will, troubled Christians may resign themselves to God's apparent indifference to their discomfort. Others may simply reject God altogether. I know of a Christian woman, regarded by her friends of many years as mature in her faith, who, after an unwanted and painful divorce from her adulterous pastor husband, gave up Christianity and declared herself an atheist. Now married to a nonbeliever, a wealthy, moral man who treats her well, she angrily tells her Christian friends, "I'm now enjoying the life I've always wanted that your God never gave me."

That woman never became aware of her deepest desire that only God can satisfy, the desire that centers in forgiveness and transformation into the kind of woman she was created and designed by God to be.

If she were to read this last sentence, I presume she might respond, "I know the verse in John 7 about living water that quenches some alleged deep thirst in people's souls. And I know Christ said He would give it to anyone who came to Him thirsty for that water. Well, I want you to know He never even gave me a sip. I'm happier without Him."

Most Wanted

Let me now introduce an assumption that, if true, and if thought through, will give each of us, including the woman now happy away from God, reason to trust God's love in any trial, no matter how severe.

The assumption:

God longs to give us precisely what we most want. What the Spirit guides us to most want that will be satisfied in this life is rich, but it is less than what the Spirit designed us to most want that will only be satisfied in the next life. He wants to give us both, each in its own time. And He will.

As you read the above words, I think you might respond in one of three ways.

> **Option 1**: If you don't understand the plot of the larger story God is telling, if you fail to grasp what in His goodness He is up to now and what awaits every Christian in the next life, you will likely dismiss the assumption with a cynical chuckle, treating it as religious Christianese with neither substance nor relevance.

> **Option 2**: If on your spiritual journey you have not yet learned to hate sin more than pain, you may still welcome the assumption, thinking you believe its message. But when difficulties come that make you more intensely aware of pain than sin, you will retreat from the assumption and not think about it while you go on doing what you can to manage your life, to restore blessings and lessen your pain.

> **Option 3**: If your gaze is fixed on God's larger story with knowledge and wisdom, you will accept the opportunity to follow the direction of the assumption's teaching that leads into choppy waters, confident in hopeful anticipation that you're becoming who you most long to be.

As I live my life now, before I die, my deepest desire for what God eagerly yearns to give me *then* will be experienced *now* as an inconsolable longing. Lewis writes:

The Christian says, "Creatures are not born with desires unless satisfaction for those desires exist. A baby feels hunger: well, there is such a thing as food. A duckling wants to swim: well, there is such a thing as water. . . . If I find in myself a desire which no experience in this world can satisfy, the most probable explanation is that I was made for another world. If none of my earthly pleasures satisfy it, that does not prove that the universe is a fraud. Probably earthly pleasures were never meant to satisfy it, but only to arouse it, to suggest the real thing."[5]

In another place, it was Lewis who coined the phrase "inconsolable longing" to mean the desire that only heaven will satisfy.

I long for everything to be *as it should be* in a world created and governed by an infinitely good and powerful God. I want to enjoy a perfectly intimate relationship with God that is now impossible due to my imperfection. I want to relate to others with the same passion and motivation with which the three members of the Trinity relate to one another. I want to live in a world with no poverty, no refugee camps, no terror threats, no war, no jealousy, and no illness. I want death and sorrow and crying and pain all to be gone, along with even the urge to sin. That, and much more, defines my inconsolable longing, and probably yours.

But perhaps there is now in me a *consolable longing* for a kind of pleasurable satisfaction that arouses my desire for what will be mine to enjoy in heaven, the inconsolable longing in my soul that available pleasures now were never intended to satisfy. Perhaps there is within me now, before I die, a desire for satisfaction that only God Himself and not His blessings can provide. The wished-for blessings of life, such things as good health, good family, good friends, and a good job are sometimes provided by God, but none are guaranteed or permanent.

Is there something we can meaningfully and profoundly enjoy now that depends entirely on the twin truths that God exists and, because of grace, He is present with us?

Something sustaining and energizing is available now in the midst of my troubles as a tempted, failing, inadequate, and weak person living in a world where dreams shatter, where safety is uncertain, where good times never last. What we can count on the sovereign God to give us now will bring with it joy and purpose and stability in the middle of good times and bad. It is the satisfaction of our consolable longing, what we wish for that can be ours, in this life.

But what I most want is to live in an unfallen world full of God's creative beauty, and to live as a person so aware of God's love that, together with others, I can love God and others with no mixed motives. That will be heaven. Until then, we live in a fallen world still stained by self-centeredness, aware of a desire that cannot be fully satisfied in this life. That desire is my inconsolable longing.

And yet joy is available now, never pure but *real*. The desire planted in my redeemed heart by God's Spirit to love well is my consolable longing, and it can be meaningfully if not perfectly satisfied now to the degree that I obey Christ's command to love others as He loved us (see John 13:34).

More than a dozen times now I've asked the question: In this life, what is God good for? I know of no other question whose answer is more misunderstood and less appreciated. In simplest terms, the answer is this: no matter how difficult and painful our lives, we can delight the Father by putting the love of Jesus on display by how we relate to others, and we can do it in the energy of the Spirit.

In this life, God can richly satisfy our consolable longing, which is the desire to love well.

"What is God good for, in this life?" Answer? The wonderful satisfaction of our consolable longing now, but only as we tremble and trust. What, then, can I happily anticipate God will do for me now?

What is our consolable longing? The answer to that question, when grasped, embraced, and celebrated, will lead us to the abundant life Jesus came to give. To understand its unexpected power, the answer requires further thought.

I can only hope someone provided a biblical answer for Jackie Kennedy after John Kennedy died. I want to know the answer for myself, and I want to share it with others.

13

The Consolable Longing

God's Provision for the Good Life That Every Christian Most Wants

Without the example of those who have gone before, proving it is possible to finish well, to tremble when God's ways make no sense and yet to steadfastly trust that His ways are good, the temptation to resist and run or distort and deny would be far more difficult to withstand.

Keep on asking, and you will receive what you ask for. Keep on seeking, and you will find. Keep on knocking, and the door will be opened to you.

Matthew 7:7

Matthew 7:7 presents an obvious problem to the minds of Christians. These are the words of Jesus, and His followers profess to believe every word He said. But in this verse, Jesus is telling us something that does not ring true in our experience. What, then, are we to do? We cannot dismiss His words. Have we misunderstood what appears to be plain enough language? Perhaps.

How often have you asked God for something important to you and never received it? In earlier days, and still recently, I have heard preachers tell me that God always answers prayer, sometimes with a no. Whether true or not, that response strikes me as a convenient way to shut down hard questions. Have you ever earnestly sought after an understandably much desired blessing and never found it? Are you to keep on seeking? For how long? What door have you persistently, even desperately, knocked on that never opened? You might expect an uncaring judge to keep the door closed. But your loving Father? Shouldn't we expect better of Him?

We all have our stories. At His invitation, we've all come to God for something and received nothing, leaving us trembling in confusion and disappointment. What Jesus said in the verse above led us to expect an outcome that never happened. It can be tempting, even for devoted Christians, to then shove our doubts and questions into a crowded closet, lock the door, and get on with our Christian lives. But if we never open the door, rummage about in the closet, and push aside the mounds of dirty clothes, we won't find the treasure hidden in a corner beneath the unwashed laundry.

Two Mistakes

By entering that closet, we admit that we might be wrongly responding to our Lord's words. We might be making two mistakes. The more common one feels so naturally reflexive that it is difficult to recognize as a mistake. The first mistake is to confidently ask God for the good things of life that provide comfort and make us feel good and, as we pray, to trust Jesus to honor what He promised. We think we understand what He was saying to us in the Matthew passage. It's obvious. We ask, and He gives. We seek, and in His

160

loving providence, we find. We knock on a door that leads to what we want, and He opens it.

It may not occur to us that granting our requests might not advance the story God is telling. Doing so might even get in the way. Could God's good story include our suffering? Unthinkable. So we continue to ask, seek, and knock, trusting Jesus to do what He said—to bless our life as we long to have it blessed.

But sometimes He doesn't. Our confusion makes us think. Did Jesus promise to provide the abundance of blessings we want that would make our lives easier and happier? Or did He not? On the face of it, the Matthew passage tells us He did. Thinking that we're honoring His Word, we therefore stifle our doubt, shelve our questions, and keep trusting God for what we want. Mistake number one.

Another mistake is often committed by more mature believers. As Christians grow deeper in our faith and become more keenly aware that enjoying God is our greatest and promised good, we can identify our desire to experience a rich sense of God's tender presence, rich enough to calm our fears, quiet our groaning, and fill us with imperturbable joy. With eager thirst to know God, we ask, seek, and knock, expecting to experience what will never be ours to fully enjoy until heaven. We may, however, faithfully practice spiritual disciplines, opening our empty souls to be filled with His felt presence, *more eager to experience Him than to delight Him.*

That's also a mistake. It centers in our refusal, conscious or otherwise, to embrace the emptiness we feel when we are in touch with our inconsolable longing. It's difficult to embrace our emptiness as an opportunity to delight God by continuing to serve Him in our dryness. We fail to accept the truth that no spiritual effort will fully yield what we most want. The longing for the joy of heaven is inconsolable till we are there.

Mistake 1: Trust God for the good life of maximum blessings and minimal trials, for what you assume is the abundant life that

Jesus promised. If life goes well, ask for nothing more. Believe that you have arrived in a place Paul never claimed to reach. If life goes poorly, *either* continue to wrongheadedly ask, seek, and knock, believing God will provide what you want, an **untroubled life**, *or* give up on God and do all you can to manage life to your satisfaction with or without His help.

Mistake 2: Trust God for an ongoing doubt-ending, fear-crushing, heart-soothing experience of His loving presence, an experience that will continuously fill your empty soul with the fullness you long for. Trust Him to give you, now, what He will not give anyone until Christ returns, an **untroubled soul**, an inner world free of all sorrow and sadness.

Both mistakes result from a wrong understanding of Christ's words in Matthew 7:7. We will only be in a position to discover our consolable longing when we realize the arrogant foolishness of trusting God for what is not promised in this life. The consolable longing, to love others as Jesus loved us, and in so doing to delight God, is buried deep within our Spirit-invaded souls. It is a thirst that God will quench before we get to heaven, if we are prompted by that thirst to ask, seek, and knock in search of its satisfaction.

Only when we give up our expectation that God will satisfy us with heaven before we get there (our inconsolable longing) will we discover our passionate desire to love well now, like Jesus (our consolable longing).

In this chapter, I do what I can to explore the consolable longing and to encourage each of us to trust God for its satisfaction. What I now aim to do will take some work. Many of us Christians, living in our narcissistic Christian culture, remain stubbornly entrenched in our assumed right to enjoy the good life of abundant blessings from God or the good life of an abundant experience of God. We live so wrapped up in our spirit of entitlement to satisfaction on our terms that it is difficult even to envision another longing we would actually prefer God to satisfy.

~

If Jesus promised to grant neither an untroubled life nor an untroubled soul, are we then to resign ourselves to the dismal thought that there is no longing within us that He guarantees to satisfy before we die? Or is there a consolable longing buried in our depths, placed there by the Holy Spirit, that can be brought to Jesus with confidence that He is eager to provide its satisfaction? If so, it would be important to understand that its satisfaction could keep us trusting God's goodness during hard times.

A brief look at a few followers of God who lived the good life *as God defines it*, a life that can be lived only when God satisfies our consolable longing, might help us understand what that longing is. The writer to the Hebrews told us to "Remember your teachers who taught you the word of God. Think of all the good that has come from their lives, and *follow the example of their faith*" (Heb. 13:7, emphasis mine).

The men and women I now want to mention (there are countless others) lived the good life that, whether we realize it or not, every one of us most wants to live. And yet too many of us think that a life abundant in pleasurable blessings or rich spiritual experiences is available now. And that is the life we think we most want, the life we trust God to provide that will satisfy the thirst we most long to quench as we live in this troubled world. Too often, we are aware of no desire for anything more. We find it easier to desire the satisfaction available in either of those two versions of an abundant life than to long for the hard-won joy of living well in the midst of crushing difficulties. Living well: delighting God by loving well.

I wonder how many of today's Christians across the world will enter their last days on earth still unaware of their consolable longing, unaware that its satisfaction would have enabled them to live

163

the fruit-bearing life that God saved them to live on their way to heaven. Because an example can sometimes bring words to mind for a reality that is difficult to describe, I want to look at seven people whose lives reflect what is possible when our consolable longing is aroused and satisfied.

Seven Illustrations of Consolable Longing Satisfied

1) Abraham

This hero of faith left a good life at home when God told him to pack his bags without knowing where God would take him. Through many hardships, discouragements, and one terrible test—God instructed him to kill his son—something survived in Abraham, something good. He endured every trial God arranged for him to experience without intractably resisting God and running from Him and without distorting or denying what he heard God call him to do. Even when he failed badly, Abraham trembled at God's ways but eventually trusted His good intent. Something survived in Abraham's soul. Something good.

2) Moses

In his prime, this leader of God's people left behind the pleasures of a lavish lifestyle; for forty years he lived a simple shepherd's life. Then for forty more years he endured never-ending trials as he led two million whiny people, all chosen by God, through an inhospitable wilderness on their way to a better place. And yet, by God's design, Moses died before entering the promised land, never enjoying the hoped-for reward for his labor. Like every follower of God, Moses failed. But through it all, he did not resist and run. He did not distort God's plan into something more comfortable, and he did not deny that God's plan was difficult. Something survived in Moses that kept him trembling and trusting till God took him to his eternal reward.

3) *Hannah*

This godly but barren woman was subjected to regular humiliation from Peninnah, her husband's other wife, a child-bearing woman who cruelly taunted Hannah for being childless. Eventually, after a long season of misery, God heard Hannah's cry. She gave birth to Samuel, a healthy baby boy, and happily declared, "I asked the LORD for him" (1 Sam. 1:20). She asked, and God gave. But God had something far better in mind for her to celebrate. When Samuel was weaned, Hannah gave him "to the LORD," wanting her son "to belong to the LORD his whole life" (v. 28). From his toddler years on, Samuel lived in the home of Eli, Israel's high priest. Hannah then visited her son only once a year, a heavy price for a mother to pay. It is remarkable to notice that Hannah sang her song of deepest joy not when she gave birth to Samuel, and not as she nursed him, but when she sacrificed the joy of motherhood for the abundant but painful joy of surrendering her son to God's purpose for him. Through barrenness, humiliation, conception, and surrender, something survived in Hannah, something pleasing to God. She trembled and trusted in the strength of what survived (see 1 Sam. 2).

4) *Esther*

This unlikely queen of Persia, wife to a sexually addicted pagan king, was a God-honoring Jewish young woman whose physical beauty made it possible for her to serve God's purpose for His people. She stepped into an uncomfortable, never-expected, and never-wanted opportunity to advance the script of God's story by becoming a queen to an ungodly king. Through circumstances sovereignly controlled by God, something survived in Esther that empowered her to live the good life of honoring God's purpose for her existence. She was "made queen for just such a time as this" (Esth. 4:14). She neither resisted nor ran from the high calling of God. There was no distortion or denial of that calling. Esther trembled at God's difficult plan for her life but trusted that God had a good outcome in mind.

5) Jeremiah

The weeping prophet (as he is commonly known, and for good reason) was called by God to a ministry that terrified him; to a ministry that required him to predict and then witness the slaughter of Jerusalem's citizens, his brothers and sisters, and the exile to Babylon of God's people who were not slaughtered; to a ministry that produced no results visible to Jeremiah. The young prophet tried to squirm away from the difficulties he knew would come his way if he obeyed God's call, but he did not resist or run. He went. As expected, he suffered. But he never distorted his understanding of God's call into something more agreeable. And he never denied the call to hardships. More than any other Old Testament prophet, Jeremiah lamented in the strongest possible words the difficulty of what God called him to endure. Still, something survived in him through his bitter tears. Jeremiah finished well, still trembling, still trusting.

6) Paul

The apostle to the Gentiles paid an uncommonly high price to trust God, a price higher than most devoted followers of Jesus today are required to pay. He was gratefully conscious that his endurance through suffering was meant by God to encourage others to similarly endure. "Even when we are weighed down with troubles, it is for your comfort and salvation! For when we ourselves are comforted, we will certainly comfort you." To what end? "Then you can patiently endure the same things we suffer" (2 Cor. 1:6). During his final days on earth, after many trials and hardships, Paul lived in a Roman dungeon, alone and awaiting execution for the crime of following Jesus. Sitting in his cell, he wrote these words to Timothy, his son in the faith: "I have fought the good fight, I have finished the race, and I have remained faithful" (2 Tim. 4:7). In earlier days, as we saw in chapter 3 of this book, Paul, then known as Saul, distorted God's Word into news that sounded good to his proud Jewish mind, into a plan that would prevent trouble in his life and allow him to feel powerful and visibly significant. But after he met Jesus, for more than thirty years Paul lived as a faithful disciple of his Lord. With his eyes opened by God to see good news that overshadowed all the necessary suffering, he neither resisted God nor ran from Him. And he never again distorted the good news of the gospel into news more agreeable to his desire for an easier life, nor did he deny the rugged truthfulness of God's good news. Something survived in Paul, something that empowered him to live the abundant life of suffering for Christ. Paul trembled, "pressed on every side by troubles, but . . . not crushed . . . perplexed, but not driven to despair" (2 Cor. 4:8). Whatever it was that survived in Paul freed him to live the good life of journeying on the narrow road.

7) *My Father*

Dad's life is a story of blessings mingled with great loss. He lost his father to the flu epidemic of 1917 when he was a five-year-old child. He lost his oldest son (my only sibling) to a plane crash in 1991. Dad earlier had lost his only brother to cancer. In his elder years, he lost his wife to six years of advancing Alzheimer's. My father was a private man, British by background and temperament. But in one rare moment, then in his eighties, he quietly said to me, "My life was hard." But he never closed his Bible. He never stopped celebrating the Lord's Supper every Sunday. He struggled mightily but never resisted and ran, never distorted and denied. Something survived in the deep places of his soul. My father fought the good fight; he finished the race; he remained faithful to the end. He trembled, even on his deathbed, but he trusted. A decade before he died, he woke up suddenly from a sound sleep in the early hours of the morning with two words forcefully repeating themselves in his mind: *sheer delight*. God gave him a vision, the last of three he was given during his eighty-four years of following Jesus before he died. In this vision my father saw his father, whom he had last seen more than seventy years earlier. "Papa," he asked, "what's it like up there?" He then heard his very-alive father reply, "I don't want to ruin the surprise. It is good beyond telling." Dad went back to sleep. Whatever had survived in him up to that time gathered new strength as he faced his final years.

I remember these stories, and many others. They intensify my desire to finish well. And yet I'm tempted every day to compromise, to place priority on my immediately felt sense of well-being. The opportunities are many. Some are difficult to resist, and some are difficult to recognize as self-centered and not Christ-honoring. The temptation feels strongest when troubles plague me that I know God could prevent, and I strongly wish He would.

In those moments, I think of Ezekiel's words. Though feeling "bitterness and turmoil," he reported that "the LORD's hold on me was strong" (Ezek. 3:14). It seems clear that all seven of these men and women—Abraham, Moses, Hannah, Esther, Jeremiah, Paul, and my father—knew bewildering disappointment and severe hardship in their lives, but they also knew the Lord's hold on them was strong.

What was it that held them? At least this: in response to trembling over God's thoughts and ways that were not committed to their comfort, each one looked deep into their soul, wanting to find the power that would keep them faithful and enduring to the end. They seemed to have discovered within them a strong thirst, a desire that was stronger than any other in the moments of difficulty and temptation, *a thirst to endure*, trusting that beyond what they could see, a good story was unfolding even in the worst of times, a story with an ending so good that all the trouble necessary to get there was worth it.

In each of them, something survived: something good, something aroused by God's Spirit. It was *the consolable longing*, a longing to endure hard times and to still love well, always with the hope of what lies ahead. In simplest terms: *a longing to persevere through every good time or bad with an undiminished, growing capacity and desire to love both God and others.*

Our inconsolable longing, for everything to be as it should be in a loving, holy, sovereign God's universe, leaves us groaning inwardly with unsatisfied desire as we wait eagerly for every desire in our redeemed, image-bearing souls to be alive with unending joy.

But our consolable longing, to faithfully endure all that is wrong in ourselves and in the world until all is made right, just might be the longing Jesus had in mind when He promised to answer prayer. If so, then we are to *ask* God to satisfy our longing to endure trials without quitting, to *seek* all that we need to stay the course on the narrow road to life, and to *knock* on the door that opens onto a reservoir of strength to trust the goodness of His sovereign plan, even when troubles come and friends disappoint. Jesus endured the cross knowing His suffering accomplished the purpose He shared with the Father. We can endure our trials for the same reason.

It will then be true that we will receive what we ask. We will find what we seek. The door will open to what we most want. Our sovereign, in-control God will see to it.

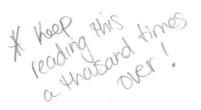

* keep reading this a thousand times over!

14

Would We Prefer to Trust
a Heavenly Grandfather?

(Is That What We're Doing?)

What would really satisfy us would be a God who said of anything we happened to like doing, "What does it matter so long
as they are contented?" We want, in fact, not so much a Father
in heaven as a grandfather in heaven—a senile benevolence who,
as they say, "liked to see young people enjoying themselves,"
and whose plan for the universe was simply that it might truly
be said at the end of the day, "a good time was had by all."

C. S. Lewis[1]

Have you ever wondered, as I have, if the sovereign God could
have come up with a better script, a more pleasant one, for
the story He is telling? So much warfare, so many heartaches, so
few really good relationships: Couldn't God's loving power arrange
for things to move along more smoothly? We like the end of the

story—heaven forever. And we are properly, though never sufficiently, grateful for what Jesus did to guarantee our never-ending and always overflowing satisfaction of what for now is our inconsolable longing. We were designed by God to enjoy Paradise, sinless people living in a garden without weeds; together among the trees, flowers, and streams of living water, enjoying the intimate presence of our loving Father thanks to our still nail-scarred Savior; so full of the Holy Spirit that divine love flows from us into others. Paradise will be ours—then.

What about *now*, before then? Must life be so difficult? His plan for now is not easy. It wasn't meant to be. But why? What I suggested in the previous chapter might really be true. God does not promise to protect us from all that we fear. Instead, He promises to satisfy a desire to delight Him by trusting His love to a sufficient degree that we gratefully endure every hardship that comes our way before we die. The trick is for us to get in touch with that desire. A good start might be to really believe, and to seriously think about, what Peter told us: life's trials are designed to show that our faith is genuine, though sometimes they reveal a faith that needs bolstering. Peter said that "When your faith remains strong through many trials, it will bring you much praise and glory and honor on the day when Jesus Christ is revealed to the whole world" (1 Pet. 1:7).

Is that what I most want now, praise and glory and honor—then? Is the consolable longing to endure difficulties now stronger than my desire to overcome difficulties and enjoy a less-troubled life? Does that longing even exist in us? Is such a desire lodged somewhere in our alive-to-God souls eagerly waiting to be aroused as we keep walking the narrow road to life? Shouldn't there be something more appealing that we can count on God to provide than the power to persevere patiently in trembling trust and to love well through all kinds of trouble that God neither prevents nor ends?

Admittedly, it is a stretch that our not yet fully renewed minds resist, but bedrock maturity, the maturity God's Spirit is developing in us, the maturity from which every Christian virtue flows, might actually be the divinely enabled ability to love Christ in the worst of times. And that would mean to never quit on Christ when it seems eminently reasonable to do so, and to never settle for managing our way into a life more easily enjoyed than endured.

That understanding of maturity, if we embrace it, puts to death every version of the health-and-wealth gospel, both the blatant version that trusts God for physical health and material prosperity and the more subtle version that promises soul health dependent upon a continuous experience of spiritual wealth, the satisfying and lasting experience of God's intimate presence that relieves loneliness, fills emptiness, and prevents failure.

Paul provides no support for either conception of Spirit-empowered maturity. He prayed that we would be "strengthened with all his glorious power," for what? So that we might enjoy life's blessings or experience God's presence? I could wish it were so. But listen to Paul's words: "We also pray that you will be strengthened with all his glorious power *so you will have all the endurance and patience you need*" (Col. 1:11, emphasis mine). Endurance and patience are needed only when trouble comes.

Paul made it clear, by both example and teaching. The Christian life requires followers of Jesus to endure hardships that God could prevent but doesn't, even when we pray. Must we then conclude that God arranges for the difficulties He wants us to endure? Does He cause them? Even the thought that He might drives us to cling to a heavenly grandfather who would do no such thing. And yet we're told to "Be thankful in all circumstances, for this is God's will for you who belong to Christ Jesus" (1 Thess. 5:18). Are we to be thankful in all circumstances because God controls all circumstances, including both disappointing and devastating ones, giving us the opportunity to show that our faith is genuine? Could that be true of our heavenly Father?

173

Two Options

I see only two possibilities. Either God is actively responsible for leading you to the spouse who broke your heart, for the cancer revealed in your routine blood test, for your son's or daughter's resistance to spiritual things, for whatever trouble has come your way—or God actively permits every troubling circumstance for a good purpose beyond our ability to fully appreciate. A deist, of course, doesn't bother with such questions. Deism holds that God neither causes nor permits life's hiccups. Long ago, says deism, God created everything, set the world in working order, then removed Himself from any involvement, and now He is living "up there" while we struggle "down here."

It sometimes appears that deistic thinking might be true. But it is bad theology. No Bible-believing Christian can accept that view. Jesus promised to never leave us nor forsake us. It is inconceivable that the Lord who endured Calvary would fail to keep His word. In some fashion, He is with us, and He has made it possible for us to remain with Him. What, then, are we to think when the world that He holds in His mighty hands is falling apart—when it is our little world that is falling apart?

Throughout eternity, our sovereign God will see to it that everything is perfect. Until then, from the fall in Eden's garden to Christ's second coming, our sovereign God sees to it that everything is useful for His good purpose; He remains in control of the story He is telling.

If we believe God is with us, still in control and always loving us, we have only two ways to think. One, our heavenly Father is actively causing everything that happens, or two, He is actively permitting everything that happens. Faith in the Bible's God allows no other option. At the moment, I find the question personally important. I am living through a season that seems spiritually sterile. I believe much. But right now little excites me. The well of living water seems to have gone dry. Has God sovereignly brought this season to me?

Or is He simply permitting it to afflict me? Which is it? Either way, I still feel dry.

The answer does, however, make a difference, a slight difference in how I view God. A God who causes struggle is difficult to trust, let alone enjoy. It seems a bit easier to trust that a God who permits struggle might have a good reason for doing so. But, of course, a God who causes trouble might also have good reason for the difficulties He brings. Either way, I would prefer to think of God as my heavenly grandfather. Bless me! Heal me! Give me the good life I so badly want. But reality makes that hope difficult to entertain. I am left with a troubling question: Is everything I see around me and in me part of the most benevolent script our sovereign God could write for the story He wants told?

It is clear that God hates divorce. He said so. "'For I hate divorce!' says the LORD" (Mal. 2:16). And yet divorce courts are full every day. I find it difficult to believe that God causes what He hates. And He hates everything wrong in the world. When Jesus stood at the grave of Lazarus and saw his sister Mary weeping, John tells us that "a deep anger welled up" in Jesus (John 11:33). God hates my cancer. He hates your insomnia. He hates whatever makes life difficult. If He really does hate our suffering, why doesn't He do more about it?

If He does not cause our suffering but for good reason merely allows what He hates, then still more than a little faith is needed to gratefully trust His unfailing love through sovereignly permitted troubles.

It is true that our heavenly Father, the Father who loves His Son through all eternity, caused Christ's suffering on the cross. Isaiah tells us with prophetic foresight that it was God's "good plan to crush [Jesus] and cause him grief" (Isa. 53:10). And God was actively responsible for seeing to it that Babylon destroyed Israel. Habakkuk could make no sense of that. Are we now to experience peace in the presence of a sovereign God who at least sometimes does cause difficulties to come our way? The difficulties He does not cause, if

175

because at that point on the cross Jesus became sin itself!

there are any, He obviously permits. Whether sovereignly caused or sovereignly permitted, difficulties still plague our lives.

It would require little creative talent to write a better script for a story sovereignty could tell. And I have done exactly that. So have we all. I call it our smaller story. Its plot makes sense to us. We think it should make sense to God. Without realizing it, we then trust a heavenly grandfather to approvingly smile on and cooperate with the plan we've come up with. From our earliest days, with a foolish nature that values our immediate well-being above all other goods, we go about crafting a story that begins at our birth and ends at our death. With no thought of a next life so good that it makes all suffering in this world actually seem little, we coauthor with God a story that calls for His sovereign, freely, and wisely chosen cooperation to provide whatever will honor our supreme value: a good life of blessings. Our part is to please God by how we live. His is to see to it that our lives follow the script we've written.

Paul joined a different story. Writing from prison and awaiting execution after living a deeply holy life riddled with adversity, Paul tells Timothy, "I have been sent out to tell others about the life [God] has promised through faith in Christ Jesus" (2 Tim. 1:1). He then writes, "With the strength God gives you, be ready to suffer with me for the sake of the Good News" (v. 8). Later in the same brief letter, he reminds Timothy that the life promised through faith in Christ Jesus includes this promise: "If we endure hardship, we will reign with him" (2:12). Toward the end of his letter, Paul simply states, "Don't be afraid of suffering for the Lord" (4:5).

One thing seems clear: the life promised to us as Christians is different from the life we would naturally expect our loving and sovereign God to provide. Perhaps we have a view of sovereignty that needs revision. Keep that thought in mind.

The psalmist wants us to know that the sovereign God "is in the heavens, and he does as he wishes" (Ps. 115:3). As inconceivable as it seems, a right view of sovereignty, a clear understanding of the beautiful good His sovereign plan will accomplish, will stir worship even as we realize that God actually wishes us to endure hardships He could prevent. Without that right view, the sovereign God will seem to be a divine sadist, desiring our endurance of pain more than our enjoyment of comfort. We then become human masochists, people created by God to perversely enjoy the pain we're made to endure. Does that make sense to you?

Three Stories

To our trembling minds, what the sovereign God wishes to do, and what our heavenly Father therefore does, can strike us as an unkind, even unjust, misuse of sovereign power. Others before us have felt similarly. I'm thinking now of Jonah, Saul, and Habakkuk. In what sense can we understand that God was faithful to His sovereign plan in each of their lives? Perhaps we can better understand what it means to say God is sovereign if we see His sovereignty in action. It might be good to remind ourselves of why their stories are recorded in the book God wrote, the stories of three men who could make no sense of God's ways, three men who at least for a season preferred to trust their lives to a heavenly grandfather. Recognize the warning that I believe the Spirit intends us to hear as I briefly review what I wrote in earlier chapters.

God's ways made no sense to Jonah.

Through His prophet, God announced blessings would come to suffering Israel. And come they did. That made good sense to Jonah. Understandably, he wanted to enjoy the good things God had provided. It is right to do so. My wife and I just returned from a weekend away with good friends designed with nothing in mind beyond our enjoyment. For those few days, God wanted us to have a good time. Paul encouraged us to trust God "who richly gives us all we need for our enjoyment" (1 Tim. 6:17).

I imagine Jonah assumed the story would end there. Life was working. But God intruded into Jonah's good life, uninvited, and told him to leave Israel, set out on foot to Nineveh, a long walk of many hundred miles through dangerous territory, and tell the wicked citizens and king of Nineveh how they could be spared from well-deserved destruction. Nineveh was the capital of Assyria, a cruel, aggressive, and powerful nation that threatened Israel's very existence.

Couldn't Jehovah, the great I Am who chose Israel to be His people, come up with a more obviously loving plan? Wouldn't it be better if God judged Nineveh in His righteous wrath and kept Israel's blessings intact for them to enjoy with no further risk of danger from their enemy? That plan would have made sense to Jonah—a better use of God's sovereign power, a story a grandfather would tell.

God's ways made no sense to Saul.

Before he met Jesus and was renamed Paul, Saul, a religious, God-fearing Jew zealous for God's honor, was determined that Israel would enjoy their entitled place in the world as God's only chosen people. Since Pentecost, the church is Christ's bride, His dearly beloved. Are we not entitled to special protection and abundant blessings from God in this God-forsaken world? What husband would allow his bride to suffer if he could prevent it? Are we, the bride of Christ, supposed to *welcome* trouble God either causes or permits (see James 1:2)? To ensure Israel's favored place, Saul engaged in a program to eliminate opposition to Israel's deserved prominence. Do I wage war against people who deny me what I want, the justice I deserve, the respect I have earned? Saul directed his righteous anger against the blaspheming disciples of the upstart false messiah named Jesus.

Saul had what he understood to be scriptural support for his violent plan. During his days as Gamaliel's student, no doubt he read and was drawn to the words of Zechariah the prophet:

> By my power I will make my people strong, and by my authority they will go wherever they wish. . . . Any nation in the world that refuses to come to Jerusalem to worship the King, the LORD of Heaven's Armies, will have no rain. If the people of Egypt refuse to attend the festival, the LORD will punish them with the same plague that he sends on the other nations that refuse to go. (Zech. 10:12; 14:17–18)

I assume that to Saul's way of thinking, God could not have made His plan more clear. The script of God's story, as he chose to understand it, fit nicely with Saul's. Authorized by God, Saul's mission was to imprison or kill Christians. Had he not prejudged what he read in Scripture, Saul might have paused on Isaiah's words: "But it was the LORD's good plan to crush him and cause him grief. Yet when his life is made an offering for sin, he will have many descendants. He will enjoy a long life, and the LORD's good plan will prosper in his hands" (Isa. 53:10). Only blind eyes and a proud heart could fail to at least wonder if Isaiah's prophecy had come true in the death and resurrection of Jesus.

But Saul, blind and proud, distorted God's message to suit his prejudice. It was beyond belief for Saul to think that God's Messiah would be born and raised in humble circumstances and then in weakness die by hanging on an accursed tree. And for the true Messiah to love despised Gentiles and welcome them as brothers and sisters into God's Jewish family was utterly unthinkable. So Saul fiercely opposed the story God was telling. He trusted the version a heavenly grandfather would tell, with a God who would never scold his arrogant pride and would approve of the smaller story Saul wanted told. A good God would do good for His people by revealing Israel to the world as His only true people. That plan made sense. God would use His sovereign power to give Saul what he most wanted, as any good grandfather would do.

God's ways made no sense to Habakkuk.

This truly God-fearing prophet wanted God to do something about the flagrant corruption he saw in Israel's leadership, corruption that drizzled down into the lives of its citizens. Corrective discipline, severe enough to get their attention and provoke repentance, would be a good plan. But God had in mind a story with a different script. He responded to Habakkuk's desire to restore His people through discipline with His declared intention not merely to provoke repentance in Israel but to destroy Israel, to sovereignly arrange for the nation He loved to be vanquished by Babylon, a thoroughly wicked nation, more wicked than Israel. According to this historical record, we have no choice but to see that God did not simply permit hardship to come upon His people, He caused it.

Like mine would have been, Habakkuk's initial response was to question, even challenge, God's plan. "O LORD my God, my Holy One, you who are eternal—surely you do not plan to wipe us out? . . . Are we only fish to be caught and killed? . . . Will you let [Babylon] get away with this forever? Will they succeed forever in their heartless conquests?" (Hab. 1:12, 14, 17). God's plan violated nearly every idea Habakkuk had of what justice, administered by the God of holy love, should look like. Shouldn't the Holy One, whose sovereign power enables Him to do as He wishes, destroy Babylon, knowing they are not His people, and merely discipline Israel, His chosen people, in redeeming love?

Habakkuk's plan would seem to be more just, more becoming of a good God. A grandfather left alone with his grandchildren would discipline them if they became unruly, but surely with the loving intent to see them enjoy the fruit of a life lived well, never to devastate them with merciless punishment. To rephrase Habakkuk's thinking in today's terms, shouldn't our efforts to please God, to spouse well, to parent well, to friend well, to work well, and to minister well be met with the success we want arranged for us by a God of sovereign love? Anything less makes no sense to our understanding of fairness.

Beneath all our resistance to trusting God when His ways make no sense and leave us trembling is one question: *What does it mean to believe that God is sovereign?* If, in church, a pastor asked his people to raise their hand if they believe God is sovereign, most, if not all, Christians would do so. If he then invited ten people who raised their hands to come to the pulpit and express what that truth means, I would expect eight would say, "To be sovereign means that God is in control of everything." Two might respond, "I'm not so sure. I guess He is in control of some things, but given what I see going on in my life, in my friends' lives, and in the world, it's hard for me to believe He controls everything that happens." One of the two might add, "My son just died in a car accident that wasn't his fault. I can't believe God killed him."

There are two views of God's sovereignty embraced within different circles in the community of Christians. After explaining in simple terms what each view holds, simple because I can do no better, in chapter 16 I will present a third view that I think meets two standards: one, and most importantly, it is supported by Scripture; and two, it frees us to more fully and gratefully worship our sovereign God, to actually like Him no matter what happens in our lives.

15

Enjoying Our Sovereign God

"The Whole of History Is Nothing More Than the Story of God's Activity"

Dietrich Bonhoeffer warned us against "cheap grace." Perhaps today's Christians need to be warned as well against cheap sovereignty—trusting the sovereign God of love to grant us whatever good we think we need to experience joy in following Jesus.

"The whole of history is nothing more than the story of God's activity."[1] Really? Is that sentence true? If so, is its author, Jean-Pierre de Caussade, the great French spiritual director who guided others toward the enjoyment of God in the 1700s, saying something we need to hear today? Among other things, it appears he is suggesting that to believe God is sovereign is to believe that He is the active cause of everything that happens across time, throughout the world, and in each of our individual lives.

C. S. Lewis shared a similar view. When his brother, Warnie, was admitted to an Oxford hospital after a ten-day bout of drinking, Lewis acknowledged in a letter written to his friend Arthur Greeves that things were "much darker than I feared." But then he added, "Don't imagine I doubt for a moment that what God sends us must be sent in love and will all be for the best if we have grace to use it so. My *mind* doesn't waver on this point; my *feelings* sometimes do."[2] Lewis trembled in the darkness and trusted God's love in the light of truth.

In his unwavering mind, Lewis apparently remained confident of three things: (1) God had sent this dark hardship into his life; (2) God sent it as an expression of His love; (3) God's love was wrapped up in His good purpose. Three familiar questions come to mind: (1) When we say God *sent* a trial into our lives, could it be that He *allowed* it, or must we assume He actively *caused* it? (2) If difficulties in our lives (perhaps tied to unanswered prayers) are truly an expression of God's love, are we then correct in saying that divine love is committed not to our presently felt comfort but rather to the enjoyment of our eventually realized well-being? (3) What good purpose that we can appreciate is served by a dark trial worse than we feared?

It takes little faith to believe that every good thing that shows up in our lives is God's gift to us, an expression of divine love. James told us that "Whatever is good and perfect is a gift coming down to us from God our Father" (James 1:17). In God's reckoning, could it be that what seems bad to us might be good and might do us good? Of course, we're grateful for good things. We gladly give thanks for an intimate marriage, satisfying employment, and excellent health. But Paul told us to "Be thankful in all circumstances" (1 Thess. 5:18). We're to thank God for the good He is doing in bad times? In what sense can we believe that trouble is a gift from our loving God?

The God of the Bible is sovereign, ruler of all creation, in control of all. And He is love, committed to our deepest well-being, now and forever, at any cost to Himself. Because that commitment flows from the glory of His nature, He alone is worthy of worship. Given that He is sovereign, must we then believe that our loving God is actively responsible for everything we hear on the news and for all that happens in our lives and in the lives of those we know and love? If the extreme proves the point, is God then responsible for the sexual perversion we hate and struggle against, and for the enjoyment of its indulgence? My answer? Of course not. But could we cooperate with a divine good purpose when we struggle against strong temptation, even when we yield? Of course. We can always join the story God is telling.

If everything is sent our way by divine love—read: caused by divine love—are we then to stretch our faith far enough to assume that sex trafficking, lost keys, a bipolar diagnosis, heavy rain on a day set aside for golf, or a drunk driver slamming into our car and leaving us permanently disabled all take place under God's purposefully caused and lovingly intended direction? *Or could it be that in everything God allows, much of which He hates, lies a good purpose available to seize?*

As I was writing this morning, I received word that a good friend had been rushed to the hospital with alarming symptoms. Is her husband directed by Scripture to believe that whatever news the doctor brings, whether grim or pleasing, is precisely the outcome the sovereign God chose? It is true that "the LORD sent a deadly illness to the child of David and Uriah's wife" (2 Sam. 12:15). Does it then follow that every illness in every person is sent by God, actively brought on by Him?

Whether sovereignly caused or sovereignly permitted, hardships remain hard, even with the guarantee that they bring with them a sovereignly arranged good purpose. Either way, the plot of the story God is telling is moving toward a wonderful climax. The movement is sovereignty in action. And that purpose will not reach the enjoyed fruition, not completely, until the next life. Paul made it clear that without hope of what lies eternally ahead, trembling now can lead to despair. "If in Christ we have hope in this life only, we are of all people most to be pitied" (1 Cor. 15:19 ESV). We may suffer with no relief till death. Accidents or disease may render us severely challenged and in chronic pain for as long as we live. When loved ones die, we live on with no realistic hope for Lazarus-like resurrection in this life that will bring them back to us.

The Way Forward

Face reality, live life without pretense, disavow false faith that promises life will work, and you will tremble. The only way forward into the abundance Jesus promised before we get to heaven, an abundance of endurance and patience that frees us to love abundantly in the darkness of hard times, is to trust as we tremble (see Col. 1:11). It is right to pray things will get better that will let us feel better, but it is naïve to trust that things will get better. We are to trust that in all the blessings and trials we experience, God is doing something that from His perspective is inexpressibly good.

Let me try to express the inexpressible good purpose toward which God is faithfully moving us: His Spirit is overwhelming the fallen power of self-centeredness so deeply imbedded within us with the thirst always stirring in even deeper places within us, a thirst to delight God by trusting His goodness in the worst of times. That overwhelming thirst frees us to relate in the divine energy of other-centeredness. And when we fail, as we surely will, we trust that God's love is not weakened and that His good purpose in us will yet be accomplished. Among other elements, that is God's good purpose for His children in this life. To call God *sovereign* means His purpose will be realized. More is involved in His sovereign power, but not less.

In his classic work *Abandonment to Divine Providence*, Caussade issues a strong challenge to today's Christians: "The truly faithful soul accepts all things as a manifestation of God's grace, ignores itself and thinks only of what God is doing."[3] God's sovereign activity (which is the whole of history) is either to cause or allow everything that happens, and then to prompt our trust that "God causes everything to work together for the good of those who love God and are called according to his purpose" (Rom. 8:28). Notice Paul does not say that God causes everything to happen. He does say that through what He either causes or allows God makes everything that does happen work together for the good purpose He sovereignly pursues.

Keeping in step with the Spirit, Caussade is calling us to abandon ourselves to God, to tremble over present or possible difficulties that God promises neither to fix nor to prevent, and to trust that a story worth celebrating is always unfolding. I hear the call to tremble and trust, and I am torn. In earlier books, I've written of my conviction that the gospel makes the impossible possible. Before I die, I could become a truly faithful soul, a near-mature disciple of Christ, a man who could draw others to Jesus by my love for Him and by loving like Him.

But am I interested? Am I more caught up in life going well for me? Do I long to enjoy personal freedom; to do as I choose, aiming toward whatever good attracts me the most; to enjoy whatever now, for at least a time, seems to smother the ache in my soul that will be with me till heaven? Am I assuming I can experience God's pleasure in me most clearly by enjoying the blessings He brings my way?

Or does my heart beat in rhythm with a divinely implanted desire to abandon myself to divine sovereignty? Do I long to savor God's inexhaustible grace even as I tremble at His sovereign plan? There is never a time in my life when God's commitment to His own glory fails to move Him to pursue my well-being. Do I believe that? Oh, Lord, I believe. Help my unbelief.

Sometimes I want to close Caussade's book, the Bible, too, and set aside God's call to abandon myself to Him as something to think about later, something that has little appeal in the present. I'm inexplicably but strongly drawn to retreat into my dreams of the life I "really" want: many blessings, few difficulties. I pray most fervently for the blessings I feel gratefully entitled to enjoy. My house sells. My health improves. My books sell. Family members and close friends all do well. I distort the good news of Jesus into the promise of a life that works as I want it to work, and then believe I am living the Christian life as a faithful soul.

I trust the sovereign God to bring the blessings I desire and to allow nothing that could sink me into despair. But then a quietly intense thirst to know God as I have not yet known Him constrains me to move in a different direction, a direction I strangely know I most want to follow. I find that I can neither stifle nor deny a pressing urge to explore all that the gospel makes possible during my time on earth, possibilities that weak faith wants me to believe are impossible.

The battle is on. I still live in Romans 7, too often doing the very things I hate. I live with the fear of what the sovereign God might either bring into my life or allow to unsettle me. My fear is more like Jonah's, "God, You shouldn't do that," and less like Habakkuk's, "God, I don't understand what You're doing. Your ways leave me trembling, but I trust Your goodness."

What Is Productive Trembling?

I titled this chapter "Enjoying Our Sovereign God." Not until I openly admitted to myself that not only could I make little to no sense of His ways but also too often I simply did not like what He does with His power did I then feel compelled to move into the mystery of sovereignty. The questions came rushing in.

Does God cause everything that happens? Does He cause only what He chooses to cause and sovereignly allow everything else? God is never the author of evil, but does He sometimes bring bad things into our lives for good reasons? Whether He causes or allows the difficulties we are called to endure that may challenge our confidence in His goodness, can we trust that He always is telling a good larger story we cannot see, a story with hard chapters that leave us hurting but contain a purpose that is moving toward an unmistakably good ending we will forever enjoy? Is that trust in God the basis of our enjoyment of His activities and of Him?

To enjoy a sovereign God requires that we have some clear idea of what we mean when we say He is sovereign. In the next chapter, I will be as specific as Scripture allows in my efforts to answer the question.

Outside of academic theological circles, there is little thoughtful interest in the deep truth that God is sovereign. Little effort is given to discerning what our sovereign God is doing in our world so filled with conflict, terrorism, tornadoes, and poverty and in our troubled personal lives. We're more inclined to stoically get on with our daily existence. And when trouble comes, too easily we say, "Well, God is in control. We can trust things to work out." Can we? Will they?

At some point, every one of us will have reason to tremble in the presence of a God whose way of loving us is foreign to our natural understanding of love, and whose way of looking out for our well being violates our sense of goodness. We may quiet our trembling soul beneath a veneer of smiling trust, a confidence that every trial will be transformed into blessing. Or we may simply distract ourselves from our agitated inner world by keeping busy in work, hobbies, or Christian activities. But then we waste a valuable opportunity. Trembling as we serve an unpredictable and untamable God opens the door to resisting and running, distorting and denying—or trusting, even enjoying, our sovereign God.

Trembling is good. It escorts us to a crossroad. Either we trust His goodness or we resist His plan that involves our suffering. Either we trust His plan or we distort it into one we prefer, a more pleasant plan that never introduces us to a holy God. Centuries ago, Joshua told Israel what God's Spirit is telling us today: "Choose today whom you will serve" (Josh. 24:15). Only when we hear God's Spirit will we

189

realize what it means to choose for the sovereign God who sometimes makes no sense or to choose against Him, to believe in a different god who offers a different gospel.

We must consider the following:

We will never uncompromisingly trust God for the supreme good He is doing in the difficulties we endure until first we tremble over the good we so strongly and understandably want that He is not doing.

Many of us have often sung the words, "Trust and obey, for there's no other way to be happy in Jesus but to trust and obey."[4] The hymn writer spoke truth. We will not willingly obey until we gratefully trust. And we will not gladly obey God until we enjoy the God we trust.

But this, too, must be said: we will not gratefully trust God and enjoy Him until we tremble over His ways with groaning that will not end until heaven. But trembling can backfire. Jonah trembled before his confusing God and said, "I have no interest in trusting such an unpredictable God." Without acknowledging it, I suspect Saul trembled over the Old Testament verses that undermined the convictions he wanted to hold. With a distorted understanding of God and His ways, he effectively said, "Because God is good, I am certain He will bless the life I want to lead." Neither resisting and running nor distorting and denying will produce the life we most long to live.

∼

Productive trembling, trembling that leads neither to resisting nor to distorting the unsettling story God is telling, will prove to be productive of trust when our understanding of sovereignty frees us to enjoy our sovereign God. It will not do to force our understanding of sovereignty to better allow us to enjoy God. We must accept whatever view of sovereignty is revealed in Scripture, confident that the sovereign God we meet in the Bible and therefore can meet in life is a God we can enjoy.

Think with me now about three views of sovereignty, two I challenge and one I embrace.

16

What Does It Mean to Say
God Is Sovereign?

*Three Views (What View Best Frees Us
to Enjoy Our Sovereign God?)*

As I was finishing this book, my wife fell. She broke her right wrist. Did God push her? If not, could He have held her steady? At least reduce the damage to a bruise? I do not believe God pushed her. The fall was not His sovereign choice. He could, however, have prevented either the fall or the two broken bones. He did neither. Why not? God is sovereign over all and in every moment. What does that mean? In such painful moments, what good is God?

Chapters 14 and 15 raised the above question in a variety of ways that occur to our puzzled minds when God's ways make no sense. In those two chapters, I scattered hints pointing in the direction of what I believe to be the Bible's answer. It's time now to provide that answer.

Two principal views of God's sovereignty are currently, and with some heat, bandied about in theological circles. Each claims the support of respected theologians. I have no wish to enter the debate, mostly due to my lack of formal theological training that disqualifies me from doing so. And, so far as I can see, for anyone to further raise the temperature would have no benefit.

Therefore, I am reluctant to firmly take sides and to either criticize or support those more knowledgeable than I, and I will not mention the names of scholars attached to these two views. Although not extensively, I have read arguments for both perspectives and have found much to profitably consider.

One view, more popular in Reformed company, is sometimes known as *meticulous sovereignty*. The other is commonly referred to as *open theism*. A more appropriate name, at least in my thinking, might be *contingent sovereignty*, a view more easily embraced in Arminian circles where meticulous sovereignty is challenged.

Provoked to reflect on both positions but unable to fully align with either, I propose a third view: *unthwarted sovereignty*. My purpose in writing this chapter, I should make clear, is not to arrive at a settled belief about God's sovereignty but to better understand what it means and why it is necessary and good for Christians to tremble and trust as we live with an unpredictable and sometimes seemingly uninvolved God. A brief and admittedly simplified look at each of the three views could advance that purpose. It is my hope that this discussion might help to shape a view of God's sovereignty that we nonscholarly Christians will be able to celebrate when times are pleasant or difficult, a view that, if true, will free us to enjoy God's sovereignty.

But I must be careful to avoid an easily made error. The issue with which I am most concerned is not to determine which of the three views is most user-friendly. It would be an egregious error to advocate on behalf of one view for the single reason that it best frees us to enjoy our sovereign God. The question to be asked is, *Which view does the Bible most clearly encourage me to affirm?* It is that view I want to list in my statement of faith. And then, not before, will I get around to exploring how the view I hold can help me delight in God's sovereignty.

I assume that whichever position enjoys the most biblical support will warmly resonate with our longing to gladly draw close to God. As we think about the three views of sovereignty, we need to ask which one, supported by Scripture and biblical theology, leads us to humbly tremble in the presence of a God who does whatever He wishes, sometimes with little apparent regard for our wishes, in a manner that gently draws us to trust that His loving goodness is revealed in all He does—revealed perhaps only to the eyes of faith.

Meticulous Sovereignty

Meticulous: exact, precise, thorough in every detail. A view of sovereignty that is meticulous rests on one central tenet: *everything that happens comes about according to God's intended design.* The sovereign God does not make do with what life throws at Him. He does not scramble to revise the plot of His story to better fit with the circumstances that randomly turn up. His absolute control over everything, control that attests to His mighty power, reduces His subjects to astonished awe. "Tremble, O earth, at the presence of the Lord, at the presence of the God of Jacob, who turns the rock into a pool of water, the flint into a spring of water" (Ps. 114:7–8 ESV).

The psalmist invites the earth itself and all who live on it to take courage: with God's unbounded power He cares for His people. We are to tremble in awe and trust in His care. Meticulous sovereignty assures us that by deliberate intention, and always with loving and holy design, God actively brings to pass everything that happens in our lives on His timetable, whether a raise in pay or a kidney stone.

Advocates of this first view appeal to many Scriptures to corroborate their understanding of what it means to call God sovereign. I will mention only a few, and present a perspective on each that calls into question whether the passage obliges us to affirm meticulous sovereignty is biblically supported. Excuse the length that follows. It seems necessary to make the point.

1. Even though it was Satan who "struck Job with loathsome sores" (Job 2:7 ESV), Job seems to attribute his suffering to God. When his wife challenged Job's steadfast belief in the rightness of trusting God and told him to "Curse God and die," no doubt trembling as he spoke, Job replied, "Shall we receive good from God, and shall we not receive evil?" (vv. 9–10 ESV). Meticulous sovereignty proponents suggest that Job correctly believed God was the definitive agent of his suffering.

Was Job thinking that God deliberately brings evil into a God-follower's life? James tells us that God never tempts anyone with evil (see James 1:13). Satan's intent was clearly evil. He brought trouble into Job's life, intending that it would lead him to curse God. We know that God is never the author of evil. Must we then conclude that God permitted Satan to do his wicked work, knowing that in His sovereignty, God would do a good work in Job through the suffering He allowed to torment him?

Christians agree that Satan can do nothing to God's children, and nothing in this world, without divine permission. But a question still presses for an answer: Did God actively cause Job's suffering with Satan serving as the delivery boy? Or did God actively allow Satan to do terrible things to Job for a sovereignly chosen good purpose that could have been best realized in no other way? Perhaps there is no answer. Perhaps the answer, if one can be found, makes no real difference. Either way, Job still suffered, and his suffering had a God-arranged purpose.

One more thought. Does receiving something from God necessarily imply that God brought about what was received? Or could it mean that God allowed what was received? Job's final words to God suggest the latter. After God made clear to Job that His ways were beyond human comprehension and would sometimes make no sense to mere humans, He waited for Job to speak. Job "answered the Lord and said, 'I know that you can do all things, and that no purpose of yours can be thwarted'" (Job 42:1–2 ESV). Job expressed no interest in whether God actively caused or actively allowed his troubles. But he knew that God was sovereignly active. As the psalmist put it, "Indeed, he who watches over Israel never slumbers or sleeps" (Ps. 121:4).

Only a deist, a non-Christian deist, would dare suggest that God was uninvolved in and indifferent to Job's trials. Job knew otherwise. Now that he has seen God—"but now I have seen you with my own eyes" (Job 42:5)—and before he knew God was about to end his suffering and doubly restore all he had lost, Job's focus was clear: in God's unthwarted and unthwartable sovereignty, He is able to further a wisely chosen purpose through whatever comes into a God-follower's life.

2. In Exodus, we hear God speaking to His chosen but reluctant leader-in-waiting. Moses is worried that his faltering speech— was Moses a stutterer?—would make him a poor choice to confront Pharaoh and demand that the Egyptian king let God's people go. God then confronted the trembling Moses with several rhetorical questions: "Who made man's mouth? Who makes him mute, or deaf, or seeing, or blind? Is it not I, the LORD?" (Exod. 4:11 ESV). God's words to Moses leave us no choice but to accept that God can and sometimes will exercise His sovereign power to cause people's difficulties.

Consider divine discipline. "No discipline is enjoyable while it is happening—it's painful! But afterward there will be a peaceful

197

harvest of right living for those who are trained in this way" (Heb. 12:11). No matter how deeply we believe in and enjoy God's tender love, we must not deny that God sometimes brings trouble into our lives that makes us miserable. Through Hosea, God told His people, "I will be like a lion to Israel . . . I will tear them to pieces! . . . For as soon as trouble comes, they will earnestly search for me" (Hos. 5:14–15). It is clear: trouble from God always comes with a redemptive purpose, but there are times it does come directly from God with no demonic intermediary.

In the early days of the church, Christians who took part in the Lord's Supper without recognizing the profound miracle that took place on Calvary were disciplined. Paul tells us, "That is why many of you are weak and ill, and some have died" (1 Cor. 11:30 ESV). Is it different today?

3. Sin leaves a trail. David committed adultery with Bathsheba, she became pregnant, and David was determined to hide his contemptible deed.

To make it appear to others that Bathsheba's husband, Uriah, was the father of the unborn child, David ordered Uriah to return from the battlefield where he was serving in General Joab's army. David made every arrangement for Uriah to sleep with his wife without knowing she was already pregnant, inviting him to enjoy a well-deserved break from soldiering and spend time with his beautiful wife. But Uriah refused to sleep in his home, knowing his fellow soldiers were living in tents. The king then invited him for dinner and got him drunk, hoping he could then persuade Uriah to go home and enjoy sex. Again the noble Uriah refused pleasure that was unavailable to his battle mates.

As a final resort, David commanded Joab to "station Uriah on the front lines where the battle is fiercest. Then pull back so that he will be killed" (2 Sam. 11:15). Uriah returned to battle, Joab followed

David's orders, and Uriah was killed. David seized his opportunity. He quickly brought the grieving widow to his palace, married her as an expression of generous consolation, and, in the natural order of things, Bathsheba's pregnancy soon became visible. Observers would assume that a child would be born to her second husband and that nothing immoral had taken place.

God intervened. He revealed David's duplicity to the prophet Nathan, who told David, "You are that man! . . . You have murdered Uriah . . . and stolen his wife" (12:7–9). Once exposed, David confessed his sin. But he then suffered God's discipline. "The LORD sent a deadly illness to the child of David and Uriah's wife" (v. 15). By referring to Bathsheba as Uriah's wife, God further rebuked David.

The point? It cannot be disputed. God was the direct cause of the child's death. David was the reason for the discipline, but God was the agent. Meticulous sovereignty argues that God brings trouble into people's lives. Sometimes He does. I may want to believe otherwise. Scripture won't let me. But the biblical record of God's discipline of David does not prove that all trouble comes directly from God.

4. John records a time when Christ's disciples wanted to know whose sin caused the man standing before them to be blind. They knew he had been born blind, a terrible misfortune. The disciples apparently could think of only one explanation for such a tragedy: God had judged the man for someone else's sin. As often happened, Jesus replied to a question with a disconcerting answer. "It was not that this man sinned, or his parents, but that the works of God might be displayed in him" (John 9:3 ESV).

Permit an irrelevant sidenote. Had I been that man, blind for however many years, I imagine I would have found God's ways not merely incomprehensible but maddening. At the very least, I would have thought His works were poorly timed. He could have cured me when I was a month old or, better yet, while I was still in the womb. If that blind man had any such thought, it was not recorded by John. Could he have been mature enough to value the privilege of providing Jesus the opportunity to display His Father's power? More likely, he was so overwhelmed with the miracle of sight that his years of blindness were not on his mind.

The words of Jesus that John did record make it clear that no one's sin was the cause of the man's blindness. God's holy judgment of sin was not involved. It must be acknowledged that the Lord's statement does not rule out the possibility that God did cause the man's blindness for another reason. But His words can more easily be understood to suggest that blindness, and a host of other birth defects, naturally show up in a world groaning in bondage to its corruption (see Rom. 8:18–22 ESV). The emphasis in the Lord's reply to His disciples' question shifts attention from the *cause* of a severe birth defect to its *sovereign use*.

I find no clear support in this biblical account for meticulous sovereignty. More likely, the record of this incident tells us that, in God's thinking, He is revealed to be more awesomely powerful as the sovereign God when we see that not only can He heal hardship He causes but He is also able and eager to bring good out of everything bad that happens in a corrupted world of fallen people, all of which He either causes or permits for a good purpose. I long for the maturity that counts it a privilege to suffer for the sake of delighting the Father by advancing the larger story He is telling.

5. We know that God "works all things according to the counsel of his will" (Eph. 1:11 ESV). We must be careful to notice that Paul did not say that God *causes* all things after the counsel of His will. He *works* all things toward the accomplishment of His eternal purpose. The familiar words of Romans 8:28 insist that in God's sovereign power, "all things work together for good," but only to those who endure all things knowing a

greater good is moving forward. Neither verse mandates belief that God is causally responsible for all things: God can work His sovereign purpose in the midst of anything. Oh, to know the joy of abandonment to divine providence!

6. In Isaiah, God plainly declares, "My counsel shall stand, and I will accomplish all my purpose" (Isa. 46:10 ESV). Joseph rested in the comfort of that truth. Remember his words to his wicked brothers who sold him into slavery. He was now second in command in all of Egypt, able to provide food for the starving sons of Jacob, and reunited with his brothers when he was in position to wreak vengeance on them for the suffering he had endured at their hands—all marks of divine providence. He said, "You meant evil against me, but God meant it for good" (Gen. 50:20 ESV).

Are we to understand that God provoked Joseph's brothers to "mean evil" against him? Did God provoke Cain to kill Abel? Or did He warn Cain against the evil deed Cain then willfully committed? And did God then make use of Cain's evil to reveal to later generations the long-term ripple effect of our sinful choices? *No* to the first two questions; *yes* to the second two.

Whether by divine providence God causes or allows all that comes into our lives, we're called to enjoy the good He provides and endure the bad. A biblical understanding of sovereignty helps us to do both. Isaiah points us to that understanding in the following familiar passage.

> The Spirit of the Sovereign LORD is upon me, for the LORD has anointed me to bring good news to the poor. He has sent me to comfort the brokenhearted . . . to tell those who mourn that the time of the LORD's favor has come. . . . To all who mourn in Israel, he will give a crown of beauty for ashes. (Isa. 61:1–3)

In a fallen world filled with fallen people, some redeemed but none yet glorified, with His permission much of the good God has created has been burned into ashes: marriages ending, children rebelling, Christians falling away from gospel-centered living, success breeding pride, morality before others being mistaken for merit before God, churches dividing, and wealth leading to either hoarding or extravagance, not generosity.

The Lord looks down on His once-beautiful creation, the creation He made in perfect beauty now degraded, and people made in His relational image to always live upwardly and outwardly now curved in on themselves. And He is grieved. "God saw the earth, and behold, it was corrupt" (Gen. 6:12 ESV). He has every reason and right to do away with it all. But in His holy and love-driven sovereignty, God sent His Son to die so that, together with the Spirit, He could bring beauty from the ashes of every offense and hardship we suffer.

I celebrate that truth. I marvel at and enjoy the God who Himself is that truth. I cannot embrace meticulous sovereignty. The difficulties we endure most often emerge not from God's chosen activity but from the fallen condition of both this world and our nature. And I stand amazed at God's sovereign willingness and ability, at inconceivable cost to Himself, to bring loving beauty out of dead ashes. I rest in His unthwarted sovereignty to always move His good plan forward in the midst of my doubts, wounds, and failures.

Contingent Sovereignty

Scripture could be understood to uncertainly support the view that God sovereignly brings about everything, including our troubles. In my reading, however, no Scripture *requires* belief in meticulous sovereignty. And the theology of the Bible, theology that tells us who God is and what He's about, moves me away from contingent sovereignty. Let me briefly share my understanding of that second view.

Among the truths we know about God, two are especially important in sizing up the teachings of contingent sovereignty: one, God lives above time; two, He has a purpose in all that happens in the universe He created and for every person born on earth. Open theism, the usual name for the view I am referring to as contingent sovereignty, derives its name from the teaching that God leaves the future open to unfold as it will, with neither His awareness until it happens nor a specific purpose for whatever happens.

Its advocates reason that since people have truly been given freedom to choose what we will, God cannot know what choices we will make until we make them. To believe otherwise, that God knows what each of us will do tomorrow, renders our choices inevitable and therefore not freely chosen. His free activity in responding to the choices we make is contingent on what we do, unknown to God until He decides the best action to take, if any, to deal with the result of our choices. In that action, He is sovereign, hence the label contingent sovereignty.

To open theists, it seems offensive to think that a loving God has a good purpose for the bad things that happen. A child dies. A teenage girl is raped. A man develops Alzheimer's. How can we even imagine that God has a good purpose in mind for such tragedies? Terrible things occur in our lives, due to either our fallen world or our fallen condition. They just happen. Our job is not to search for God's purpose beneath these dreadful experiences. There is none. Christians must only endure our trials, not welcome them as opportunities for great joy (see James 1:2); rather, we are to please God by neither grumbling over pointless fate nor turning away from the God who provides no redemptive purpose in our suffering. We are to live Christianly as we wait for Christ's return, when He will make everything new.

But the Bible is clear. God does have "a plan for the fullness of time, to unite all things in him" (Eph. 1:10 ESV). It is no stretch to therefore assume that in every circumstance of life the God who knows the end from the beginning (see Isa. 46:10 ESV) is moving the plan forward as the Spirit forms us to be more like Christ through all that happens.

The eternal God exists above time. Nothing catches Him off guard. But our real freedom to do what we choose tomorrow remains intact while the God who sees tomorrow as if it were today knows the choices we will then make. And His sovereign purpose for our lives, which centers on our putting Jesus on display by how we relate, presents us with the opportunity to cooperate with or oppose His purpose in every moment. Even when we fail, His matchless wisdom and lavish grace move His children toward our dazzling destiny.

Adam's failure did not surprise God. Neither does mine. He knew both were coming. And He was prepared with a plan to put divine love on display for all to see. God knows the future and has a beginning-to-the-end plan that unfolds in all that happens. I am grateful to contingent sovereigntists for challenging my thinking, but I am unable to support their position. If I were required right now to choose between meticulous sovereignty and contingent sovereignty, if there were no further option, without hesitation I would align with the former.

Unthwarted Sovereignty

Little needs to be added to this already long chapter. I have tipped my hand. The view I choose to call unthwarted sovereignty rests on four simply stated propositions:

1. *God is free to do whatever He wishes.* In His loving wisdom, He sovereignly chooses to advance the story He is telling in any way He sees fit. Sometimes His pure ways make no sense to our impure minds. But we are always the benefactors as He realizes His ultimate purpose to glorify Himself, to reveal His holy love in all His activity.

204

2. *God is always active, always up to something good.* Either God causes what happens, both trials and blessings, always for the single purpose of advancing the larger story He is telling, or He allows what happens, good things He wants us to enjoy or hard things He calls us to endure, with confidence that all things really are working together in God's mysterious sovereign ways for our deepest good.

3. *Even the wrath of man, energized by our flesh, directed by hell's wisdom, and approved by the world, will further God's eternal purpose to reveal Himself above all else as worthy of praise.* His worthiness does not center in a commitment to our immediately felt well-being. The world, the flesh, and the devil are allowed to have their influence on our lives. But He continues to reveal Himself as the source and architect of eternal beauty available nowhere else, the beauty of perfect love in action during good times and hard. His activity, the whole of history, unfailingly furthers "the purpose of his will, to the praise of his glorious grace" in saving sinners such as me (Eph. 1:5–6 ESV).

4. *The sovereign God sees to it that nothing that happens in this world, nothing that either lost or saved people can do, will thwart His purpose.* He is in total control of the story He is telling. He is the unthwartable God.

This poor man's theologizing about sovereignty reduces to one disarmingly simple and soul-comforting truth:

In all that makes us tremble, we can trust that God is doing us good.

What good is He doing? Or, to ask the question as I have before: What good is God? It is at least the following. He is stripping us of the naïve, self-serving notion that His primary goal is to make our lives pleasant and minimize hardships that make our lives difficult.

Only as immature faith yields to trust in God's unthwarted sovereignty will we welcome suffering and value the deeper good of knowing God through it. Only then can we rest in hope and enjoy His sovereign love.

~

Thoughts like these, though I believe them to be biblically derived and deeply encouraging, weary my mind, sometimes to the point of developing a bad headache.

In part 4, the final and shortest section of this book, I take a couple aspirin and think more simply about the godless stupidity of resisting and running from God or distorting and denying His good news to better match the desires of our flesh, and about the God-honoring opportunity to revel in the grace-filled invitation to tremble when God's ways make no sense and to trust that, in His superior wisdom, His thoughts and ways always reflect His love. Praise the Lord. Great things He is doing now; even greater things then.

PART 4

When God's Ways Make No Sense

Three Parables

17

A Modern-Day Jonah

"I Know Better"

The man was disappointed with God.

But he never brought his concerns to God. He never approached God with a thoughtfully open, genuinely honest, and reverently humble attitude. His mind was made up. God was wrong. He was right.

An unprejudiced observer of the man's life story, unless unusually discerning, could not have predicted his reaction. The man was brought up in a fine Christian home, albeit a somewhat nominal one, a concern only a keen observer would have noticed.

The man's parents were mostly regular in church attendance. As a boy, the man enjoyed Sunday school and, as a teen, was happily involved in a youth group. With his two sisters and mother, he faithfully bowed his head at family dinner when his father thanked God for the food they were about to eat. During mealtimes, his father was often outspoken in his defense of the Christian values to which he adhered, and he was consistent in crediting God with the family's many blessings.

The lesson was learned: *God is useful.* God was to be taken seriously as a reliable and dutiful Father who was always looking out for His children's felt interests. It never occurred to the man that he was thinking of God more as a heavenly grandfather, a doting one at that, than as the heavenly Father whose unswerving commitment to His own glory brings great hope to His followers.

The lesson from childhood, alive but never consciously articulated, continued unchallenged into his adulthood. The man met and married a lovely, godly woman more devoted to God's interests than her own. Three children were born to the man and his wife, and now, as young adults, each was living a responsible, productive, and comfortable life.

Two children were married. The third lived in New York, pursuing a career on Wall Street, too busy to add family to his life. His father was proud of his son's diligence and drive. The man enjoyed his three grandchildren, healthy and happy kids who lived close by, two fine boys and a pretty little girl. And thanks to his successful career, still ongoing and well paid, he was able to generously provide for his growing family as needed.

God was doing His job. Life was good. The man was grateful, as his father had taught him to be, thankful that God blessed His good children with good things. With his wife, he continued to be actively involved in church and faithfully contributed to its ministries.

Had the man been privy to the conversations going on in the community of God, he would have heard the Father speaking:

This man does not yet know who I am or what I am up to in his life. He is enjoying who he thinks I am the way a spoiled child enjoys the indulgence of a foolish father who wants nothing better for his child than to be happy and satisfied with the blessings of life. My heart is grieved.

The man would have heard the Son reply:

Father, both in my life and more in my death I have made known Your longing to bring people who do not know You into Your arms of holy love, the only kind worthy to be called love. It grieves Me to feel Your grief and to see the man still blind to Your gracious plan for the part he was designed to play in the story You are telling.

Had the man continued to listen, the words of the Holy Spirit would have burned with hope in his ears:

Father and Son, Your holy intent to fill this man's soul with true joy captures Me. When You allow fallen nature to take its course in this man's life, I will make him aware of the collision of two kingdoms that will then reverberate in his mind and soul. He will be brought to a many-times-over point of choice between yielding to Adam's inheritance of a God-dishonoring, entitled spirit (which till now has been his way of life) and gladly surrendering to the God-honoring spirit I will place in his soul. I long for him to join the story of grace We are telling; the story, Father, that You have scripted. For Your pleasure I want the man to dance with Us in the joy of love. I, too, am grieved, and till now quenched by his wickedly foolish understanding of what his proud, independent soul most desires. Father, You have granted free will to the man. My soul aches with longing to bring him to You. The choice will be his to make.

Willfully unaware of the divine conversation—had he immersed himself in God's love letters written to him, he would have already begun to trust God's ways—the man reflected on his life, stirred to do so by what had just happened: his eldest son, married and father of two, was diagnosed with inoperable brain cancer. Crushed by the news and angry at God, his teenage granddaughter defiantly announced her attraction to women.

God wasn't doing His job. His ways made no sense to the man.

In rattled desperation, he prayed. Dozens of church friends prayed for miraculous healing for his son. A church-organized prayer chain brought hundreds more storming the gates of heaven, pleading with God to do what surgeons could not do. The few close friends he told of his granddaughter's same-sex desire prayed that God would stir in her feminine soul a moral passion to enjoy a man.

A year had now passed. His eldest son had died a painful, terror-filled death. His granddaughter, now seventeen, had a steady girl-friend, a woman in her twenties with whom she wanted to spend the rest of her life.

On both counts, anguish filled the man's heart. He was heartbroken—and furious with God. He withdrew his church membership. In a let-ter addressed to the church elders, all longtime friends, he explained his decision with these words: "I cannot believe in a God claiming to be love who would allow such suffering in the life of one of His long-term followers. I have been faithful to Him. He has not been faithful to me. Either He is not good or He does not exist. I can no longer pretend to worship Him in church. I will get on with my life as best I can, without Him."

The man's wife was distraught, more over her husband's failure of faith than over either her eldest child's death or her granddaughter's same-sex interests. Both troubled her deeply, driving her to her knees with pleas to know God with new intimacy. Her faith supported her in the hope that God's incomprehensible ways were advancing a good story, even in the darkest night, a story with an eternally wonderful ending.

The man loved his wife and was strangely bothered by her faith. To pacify her, he continued to attend church, though less often than before and each time with seething resentment toward a God who would treat him so unfairly, a God whom he must think existed if he hated Him. *No, that doesn't follow. I don't believe He exists.*

With anger that he found disturbingly uncomfortable—*Who am I mad at? There is no God to blame!*—the man wrote in his journal: "What Christians call the blessings of God are no more than random happenings. Some people get lucky. Others don't. I'm among the unlucky ones. Fate refuses to smile on me. I accept that I will live my life as best I can, doing everything in my power to keep whatever good things remain in my life, maybe to arrange for a few more. But I'm done with God. If He exists—why am I even wondering if He does?—it's clear that He has no interest in my well-being, no interest at all in my happiness. I'm now on my own, and glad for it, free of the wish-fulfilling illusion that God is love. I know better than Him. I know better how to arrange for the life a good man such as I deserves. My life is hard, but I'll do whatever it takes to feel as good as life permits. I have no greater purpose."

The man was a modern-day Jonah, quitting on God when God's ways made no sense. The Hound of Heaven continued to bark.

18

A Modern-Day Saul

"I Can Make It Better"

The woman loved the God she imagined Him to be.

She smiled indulgently when others spoke of God's call to endure hardship and to suffer for the cause of Christ. The woman knew what it meant to suffer, more than most. She was no stranger to hardship. But she knew God, the God who promised to transform every season of trouble into a lifetime of blessings.

If only every Christian could know the Jesus she knew, they, too, would then enjoy the abundant life He came to give to all the Father's children. And, blessing upon blessing, they would know the gentle Spirit who awakened her every morning with the joy of anticipation. Life with God: What could be better?

Now, it must be understood: the woman was no romantic idealist living in the utopia of fanciful dreams. She had been four years old when her alcoholic father abandoned his wife and only child, a little girl who was devastated. She remembers crying herself to sleep every night for months, wondering what she had done to make her daddy hate her so much. Through her tears she'd prayed, "Please, God, give me a daddy who will love me."

Two years passed. Fewer tears fell from her swollen eyes, but the longing ache in her heart remained. Her prayers continued, but with fading hope for an answer. And then, in God's timing, a wonderful man came into her life. He loved the young girl's mother and seemed to love her as well. It wasn't long before the man married her mother and moved his new wife and daughter into a lovely home right next to the church he pastored.

God was good. Life was good, better than ever. On Sunday mornings the girl never wanted to leave the adults for children's church. She loved to hear her new daddy preach. Many others did as well. Older congregants believed the pastor's marriage had made him even more powerful in the pulpit. The church grew from hundreds to thousands. Life was more than good. It was exciting.

The pastor delivered every sermon from creative new angles and displayed his knowledge of Scripture by quoting many verses in the Bible to make his point. But his well-received message was always the same: *God loves you and wants you to enjoy your life to the fullest.* No sermon was complete until the pastor closed with the same inspiring words he repeated every Sunday with the warmest of smiles, words that everyone in the church waited eagerly to hear once again:

"Nights may be dark. But the sun rises every morning. Walk in the light of Jesus and enjoy the blessings He loves to provide. May His countenance brighten every moment of your day. Go with our good God into your good life."

The lesson was learned. The growing young woman understood: trust God and life works!

But the woman, now sixteen, wondered. Her mother's life hadn't worked for the nine years she was married to her abusive first husband. And yet her mother seemed to always trust God. In a quiet moment together she asked her now-happy mother how she endured those nine difficult years.

"Oh, honey, since I was a child I knew Jesus loved me. I prayed every day that God would either change that man into a loving husband or somehow free me to be a wife to a man who would love me. Sometimes you have to wait for God to answer your prayers. But remember what your father tells us every Sunday: nights may be dark. But the sun rises every morning. God brought the sun to shine on my life. His love wouldn't let Him do less."

The teenage girl smiled as she remembered her prayer when she was four: "Please, God, give me a daddy who will love me." And He had. She realized again: *gospel* means good news. A loving God can do no less than preserve His children through hard times with the certain hope that He would bless their lives with the abundance they desired. Though still in her teens, she was already a confirmed believer.

As the church grew, the youth pastor was assigned to oversee adult ministries. A new youth pastor was hired. He taught the junior and senior high school kids something they hadn't heard before. He told them that Jesus died to forgive their sins and now, as forgiven sinners with the Holy Spirit living in their hearts, they were privileged to love God and others whether their lives were pleasant or difficult.

Difficult times were to be welcomed? Welcomed as opportunities to display God's faithfulness to His good purpose by loving others? No, hard times were to be changed by God into good times. The girl was troubled. So were many parents, her dad included.

The word spread. The new youth pastor was teaching another gospel to the young people. With the support of the elders, the pastor asked him to leave. Without a fuss, and with puzzling grace, the youth pastor immediately resigned. A meeting was called. The girl's father, senior pastor of the church, spoke to the youth group. He emphasized that he loved the young man but, for the good of the church, false doctrine could not be allowed to be taught. He then encouraged the young people to pray for their former youth pastor, that he would one day come to realize that God was good.

The girl was no longer troubled. Life moved on.

Now a young woman, she graduated from the Christian college her father, with some hesitation, had encouraged her to attend. The student president of the theology club, a bright and thoughtful young man in her class, had been pursuing her for almost a year. He was drawn to her love for God. They soon married.

In his second year of seminary, she became pregnant. Together, they thanked the Lord for the welcome blessing. Months later, the baby was stillborn. The man and woman held each other and wept together. But she was angry. How could a loving God allow such a disaster? The woman wanted to be a mother. Gently, the man assured his wife that in their grief God was doing a good work in their souls, forming them to become more of the holy Christians He saved them to be, more like Jesus, who endured terrible suffering to advance the story His Father was telling, a story that included trouble till heaven.

The woman was stunned. The good she wanted was a healthy baby. Something in her snapped. Her husband was distorting the gospel. He was denying God's promise to give them a good life. How could she stay with a man who would not trust God to end her night of grief with the rising sun? She filed for divorce, praying that a truly *Christian* man would come into her life, a man with the faith to believe that a good God would satisfy her soul with a good marriage and healthy children.

In the unseen world, a world the woman had no idea existed, the Father was speaking:

The woman does not realize she is living as the daughter of Eve. She cannot conceive that in My goodness I sometimes deny to My loved ones the satisfaction of a lesser desire in order to rouse and satisfy a deeper desire in their souls that bear the image of Our community of love.

The Son replied:

218

Father, I grieve to know her eyes have been blinded by the false gospel our enemy teaches. She now is living in the hell of being unable to love anyone more than herself. She cannot comprehend that the tragedy of a stillborn child, though a terrible tragedy that We hate, is not worthy to be compared with the tragedy of a soul unwilling to live in Your love.

God's Spirit then added:

Her proud heart is trembling with anger over her misfortune. Only when her not-yet-humbled heart trembles in hope as she suffers will she be able to believe that the story We together are telling is unimaginably good. I will speak into the dryness of her thirsty soul, and into the terror supporting her pride. And I will speak with the voice of love. I have no other voice.

Years passed. The woman married a successful surgeon who professed love for the God of his wife's imagination. She was now the mother of twin boys, both healthy, and of a third child, a beautiful little girl she prayed would come to complete the good life she wanted. A good God could provide no less.

The happy family gathered every Sunday in the church of the woman's choosing, a church pastored by a man who reminded the woman of her second father, the pastor of her youth. Like him, this pastor faithfully preached the false gospel that now, more than ever, she knew to be true: *trust God and life works!* With settled passion, the woman loved even more the God she imagined Him to be.

More years passed. The woman's first grandchild, a healthy baby boy born to her happily married beautiful daughter, died in his crib. The autopsy came back: sudden infant death syndrome, an unexplained tragedy.

A few months later, when the woman was still reeling in confusion and anger over her grandson's death, which God could have prevented, her husband's long-term affair with his nurse was exposed.

219

The woman begged him to give her up and help piece together the broken fragments of her good life, whatever was left to restore. But he left her and moved in with his nurse.

The woman was inconsolable. Questions stormed through her soul. *Is God good? If so, what is He good for?* She didn't know. She was seriously asking these questions for the first time. The Hound of Heaven was barking.

19

A Modern-Day Habakkuk

"There's Nothing Better"

The man's soul was tortured.

It had been from the early years of his life. The man remembered his childhood as happy, mostly carefree and fun. But even when playing ball with his friends—and he was a good athlete—he felt strangely alone.

But not sad. Often he wanted to be literally alone, no friends around, by himself. Only then could he think the big thoughts that would otherwise lie dormant in his mind. Those big thoughts troubled him. He didn't know where they would lead. And that made him afraid. But more, they made him feel alive, alive in a different way than when a pretty girl smiled at him or when he cleared the bases with a game-winning home run. Thinking big thoughts made him feel alive in a big universe. He was often alone and feeling alive, but never often enough.

With some warmth, the man could recall the recognition he earned from his parents for living responsibly, doing his chores without needing reminders, and always making his bed before running off to school. His teachers, too, awarded him kudos for studying diligently, making good grades, and behaving well in class. But the affirming comments, though gladly received, failed to fill an empty place somewhere deep inside him, a place he later came to recognize as a yearning void, a longing without hope of satisfaction. Even as a boy, the man had lived with a tortured soul.

Like other boys his age, he labored to finish his homework early enough to watch television before bedtime. Some boys, of course, told their parents they had no homework on the night their favorite show was on the small black-and-white screen. This boy never did that. But like other boys, after lights out and his mother's whispered "Good night" as she closed his bedroom door, he would wait till the sound of her footsteps told him she was in another part of the house, then turn the light by his bed back on and read Superman comic books.

He felt alive as he fantasized flying high above the world, spotting a problem with his long-range X-ray vision, then swooping down to save the day with superhuman power. Sometimes he would put the comic book down, half read, and reach for his Bible, the one his father had given him. He didn't know why, but reading the adventures of Superman stirred a desire to read his Bible.

He kept both his thrilling Superman fantasies and his late-evening Bible reading to himself. Both brought big thoughts to mind that felt too personal to share. He feared that making them known would put him more painfully in touch with the void that never went away.

As the boy moved into his teenage years, he could sense that his father was troubled by big thoughts that he, too, kept to himself. A comment here and there told him that his dad was both troubled and enlivened by what was going on in his mind. But still his father laughed, cracking silly jokes he really enjoyed. And he liked to play tennis and would sometimes get caught up in a good western on television or a fun comedy show. How did he do it? The boy didn't know. But his father seemed to live content with the weight on his shoulders—no, on his heart—a weight that made him value time alone, most often with a Bible on his lap.

The boy longed to be with his father in those private moments, maybe even sharing big thoughts. But it felt wrong to intrude. And he was afraid. He might hear bigger thoughts than his own, thoughts that might lower wonder into despair. But somehow the teenage boy knew that despair would carry him to a place he longed to find.

The Hound of Heaven was already barking, quietly.

Life continued. And it was good. The boy's mother went about doing what good mothers do. But like her husband, she, too, seemed focused inward, oddly remote from what was going on around her. He wondered if his mother felt alone with private desires that her good life could not satisfy. And the weight that hung on his father, whatever it was, slowly grew heavier. It wasn't till the last decade of his life that, in a quiet moment, he told his son, "My life has been hard."

In that moment, the man felt closer to his father than ever before. A deep place in the father met a deep place in the son. The word *intimacy* found new meaning.

In the man's younger years, church, regularly attended as a family, was an experience to be looked forward to. What he learned, mostly from his father though supported by teachings in Sunday school, youth group, and sermons, made sense. As a teen, the man knew sin was real. He did wrong things and imagined bad things that no one suspected. He wore shame as a protective wall that only God could see through. He knew God hated sin, but he also believed that God loved sinners.

Over the years, seeing his father reading his Bible more than any other book convinced the growing boy that the Bible was an important book. He assumed that whatever it said was worthy of trust. He knew the Bible taught that God sent Jesus to die, to endure the righteous wrath of a holy God against sin, a holy loving God who

223

wanted nothing more than to forgive sinners and lead them on a path to joy, His kind of joy.

It made sense. But some things didn't make sense. God was good. He wanted people to experience joy. Why, then, all the troubles in life that He could prevent? Why the void of unsatisfied desire? Why the inability to resist favorite sins? Big thoughts became big questions.

Time moved on. It always does. The boy was now a man, happily married to a truly wonderful woman, father of three good kids, successful in his chosen career—and still tortured, longing for satisfaction he couldn't find. A terrible thought, a big one, struck him. Maybe whatever it was that would satisfy wasn't anywhere to be found in this world. His reaction to the thought surprised him. It was odd. The thought simultaneously terrified him and attracted him. To what, he wasn't sure.

Then life, as it does for everyone, got tough for the man. One of his three well-adjusted children, his only daughter who was nicely slender, began losing weight and became uncharacteristically withdrawn. His happy marriage ran into new tensions, difficult ones, not difficult enough to threaten divorce but still unsettling. Unexpected expenses stretched his finances thin.

Then the man got word that an older Christian friend, a spiritual leader who had strengthened the man's faith when it had weakened, had left his wife of more than forty years for another woman. Soon after, a decade-long friendship unraveled. And dissension developed among members of the church elder board on which he served that made cooperation difficult.

The man could not close his eyes to so much that was wrong. For years he had been living with a hopeful vision of what the gospel of God made possible: peace in the midst of turmoil, light in the darkness of night, joy blossoming from the Spirit no matter the hardships of life, strength to resist temptation, and unity within Christian community.

The question tortured him: Why were these satisfying possibilities so rarely, and never completely, realized? More than ever, the void within him ached with unsatisfied longing. Perhaps there was nothing for him but to press on, managing his troubles as best he could, enjoying whatever good things remained, and distracting himself with reliable, mostly moral pleasures that would numb the ache.

But the man could not run from the one big question that demanded an answer: *What good was the good God doing in the midst of all that was wrong?*

Uncertainty, turmoil, and confusion made the man tremble. But he did not resist the God whose ways made no sense to him, and he did not run from God into pleasurable distractions. At least not for long. The reality he faced made it impossible to distort the good news of Jesus into the promise that life's problems would all straighten out and that life's blessings would fill his void with the longed-for satisfaction. The man trembled as never before. Life required it.

But even as he trembled, without denying the anguish in his soul that he could not quiet, he sensed welcome movement within. The Hound of Heaven, revealed now to be the Holy Spirit, was inviting the man to rest in mystery.

There was, of course, no mystery in the heavenly places. The Father was smiling.

The man's soul has been opened by his trembling, trembling that is overwhelming the power of his pride. Son, the work you have done is enabling the man to flow in rhythm with the story We are telling. I am delighted.

The Son replied:

Father, I have no greater joy than to be the source of Your delight. Yes, the man is trembling, and he will continue to do so. The satisfaction We designed him to desire will live within his soul as hope.

And the Spirit added:

He is now trusting that a good story is unfolding even as he trembles in the mystery of Our thoughts and ways. How We think and what We do are beyond anything he could imagine without the light I've been sent to shine in his soul.

Strangely to the man, though not to God, the more he accepted the trembling that the thoughts and ways of God made necessary, the more he discovered faith in the goodness of God that survived all the wrong he saw in himself and others. The man rested in trust that a good story was on track in a troubled world and in his trembling soul. The real Superman was flying about, doing what He came to do.

The man continued to tremble. Some things in life improved. Some did not. Some got worse. But the man lived in the hope that trust made possible. He trusted the invisible God to make Himself visible in how the man lived and related. And he realized: there's nothing better. The man was walking the narrow road to life.

In this illustration of a modern-day Habakkuk, I have blended a few elements of my experience into the story. The "man" now walking the narrow road to life as he trembles and trusts represents a vision of who I long to become. (The two earlier illustrations are fictional. Any similarity to real persons is unintended.)

Final Comments

Unsettled Trust

As I finish writing this book, I realize I often still tremble more than I trust. Perhaps that is your story as well.

I've just reread everything I've written in these nineteen chapters. And something occurred to me that might encourage us to stay the course.

Western Christian culture appears to be divided into two groups. One group, perhaps three-quarters of us, emphasizes God's love in a way that deemphasizes God's holiness. The other group, maybe only one-quarter of us, emphasizes God's holiness in a way that deemphasizes His love.

Both belong together, each infused with the other. Dividing them has unfortunate consequences. Consider the obvious:

- Because God is holy, His thoughts and His ways are holy.
- Because God is love, His thoughts and His ways reveal love.

Emphasize God's love over His holiness and you come up with a compassionate God who wants nothing more for His followers than that they feel good about themselves and their lives. God therefore happily supports and warmly approves whatever we do that relieves distress and provides satisfaction, within broad limits of morality.

Self-examination in the light of God's holiness then becomes an unnecessary bother, a needless journey toward self-awareness. Big sins are obvious, easily recognized, and mostly avoided. Relational sins, sins that fall short of holy love, are subtle, easily ignored, and mostly committed without awareness. They are not of concern.

Self-assured confidence in God's loving thoughts and ways obscures conviction in the presence of His holy thoughts and ways. Real trembling is avoided and naïve trust is enjoyed.

Emphasize God's holiness over His love, and you come up with an austere God who demands obedience to His commands with little regard for the suffering that may be required. God therefore sternly supports and unsmilingly approves whatever we do that conforms to His rigid standards, at least the standards we lower to put within our reach.

Safe rest in the warmth of God's love becomes a luxury people who still sin cannot afford. Harsh scrutiny energizes continual self-examination with the goal of owning wretchedness that pleads for mercy in the hope of avoiding God's deserved wrath.

Conviction in the presence of God's holy thoughts and ways eliminates the joy of rest in God's loving thoughts and ways. Anxious trembling continues and restful trust proves impossible.

~

God is love and God is holy. He is the God of holy love, the God whose love never compromises His holiness and whose holiness never trivializes His love. It is this God who tells a story that requires us to tremble, because He cannot and will not allow true disciples to be satisfied with less than the depths of His holy love. Suffering is inevitable in order to combat premature contentment with a comfortably blessed life. God can and will do a good work in us that empowers us to patiently endure life's difficulties He does not prevent as we wait eagerly for the eternity of perfect joy He promised.

You and I can tremble in hope as we trust that all is well. His good story is on-track. All things are working together for a good purpose, to slowly form us into "little Christs" who display the relational, holy love of Jesus until we share in divine happiness forever.

Trembling is inevitable on the road we must walk if we are to trust that the God whose ways make no sense is always doing us good.

Notes

Introduction God's Way of Thinking Doesn't Easily Fit into Our Minds

1. G. K. Chesterton, *Orthodoxy: The Romance of Faith* (New York: Image Books, 1959), 17–18.
2. Johnson Oatman, "Count Your Blessings" (1897), public domain.
3. Louisa M. R. Stead, "'Tis So Sweet to Trust in Jesus" (1882), public domain.
4. Wendell P. Loveless, "Every Day with Jesus" (1936), public domain.

Part 1 When God's Ways Make No Sense, What Then?

1. As quoted in David Mathis, "Luther's First Thesis and Last Words," *Desiring God*, October 31, 2008, https://www.desiringgod.org/articles/luthers-first-thesis-and-last-words.

Chapter 7 A Hands-Off God?

1. Ira F. Stanphill, "God Can Do Anything."
2. Dick Lucas, *The Message of Colossians and Philemon* (London: Intervarsity Press, 1980), 77. Emphasis mine.
3. C. S. Lewis, *Mere Christianity* (New York: MacMillan, 1960).

Chapter 12 In God We Trust

1. Babbie Mason, "Trust His Heart," © 1989 Dayspring Music LLC.
2. C. S. Lewis, *The Screwtape Letters* (New York: HarperCollins, 2001), 39–40.
3. Lewis, *Screwtape Letters*, 39–40, emphasis mine.
4. As quoted in John Piper, *The Legacy of Sovereign Joy* (Wheaton: Crossway, 2000), 19.
5. Lewis, *Mere Christianity*, 120.

Chapter 14 Would We Prefer to Trust a Heavenly Grandfather?

1. C. S. Lewis, *The Problem of Pain* (New York: MacMillan, 1962), 40.

Chapter 15 Enjoying Our Sovereign God

1. Jean-Pierre de Caussade, *Abandonment to Divine Providence* (New York: Random House, 1975), 42.

2. C. S. Lewis, *The Collected Letters of C. S. Lewis: Books, Broadcasts, and the War 1931–1949*, vol. II, ed. Walter Hooper (New York: HarperCollins, 2004), 953.

3. Caussade, *Abandonment to Divine Providence*, 1.

4. John H. Sammis, "Trust and Obey" (1887), public domain.

Dr. Larry Crabb is a well-known psychologist, conference and seminar speaker, Bible teacher, popular author, and founder/director of New Way Ministries. He is currently scholar in residence at Colorado Christian University in Denver, and visiting professor of spiritual formation for Richmont Graduate University in Atlanta. Dr. Crabb and his wife of more than fifty years, Rachael, live in the Charlotte, North Carolina, area. They have two sons, both married, and five grandchildren.

Dr. Crabb continues to lead a weeklong School of Spiritual Direction several times each year and speaks at various conferences. As part of his legacy, he has recorded, and will continue to record, video series on relational issues, Bible books, and spiritual formation. For additional information please visit www.newwayministries.org.

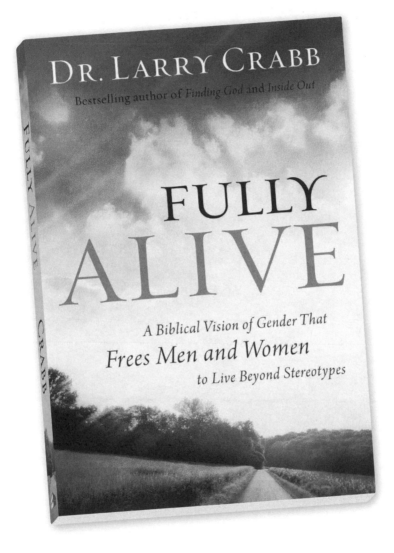

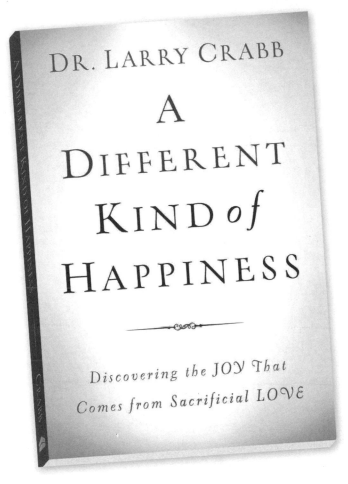

NEWWAY MINISTRIES WAS FORMED IN 2002 BY DR. LARRY CRABB.

It was birthed out of the passionate conviction that there is a new way to live made possible by the New Covenant that must become better known. We seek to introduce people to this new way of living, thinking, and relating that only the gospel makes possible. Our intended contribution to this revolution occurs through four distinct ministries:

- *Conferences*
- *School of Spiritual Direction*
- *Resource Library*
- *Internet Courses and Certification*

Dr. Crabb's work focuses on a biblical understanding of various aspects of life, such as marriage and manhood. Today, Larry is zeroing in on three topics:

- *Encounter*—what it means to experience God
- *Transformation*—what it takes to become like Christ
- *Community*—what real community is and how it helps us experience God and become spiritually formed

DR. LARRY CRABB is a psychologist, speaker, Bible teacher, bestselling author, and founder/director of **NewWay Ministries.**

Our Calling - To ignite a revolution in relationships, a new way to live that explores the real battle in our souls and frees us to value intimacy with God more than blessings from God. It's a new way that's as old as the Bible. It's what following Jesus is all about.

Our Mission - To equip followers of Jesus to *enter the battle* for the souls of those they love—the battle to resist the Old Way and live the New Way.

www.newwayministries.org
info@newwayministries.org
phone: 970.262.9110
fax: 970.468.9696